There are no Fat People in Morocco

by

Lawrence Bransby

ISBN 9781521011904

Please note: I have published this book without photographs to lower the purchase price. As we live in the digital world, I encourage you to go to www.hareti.co.uk, my son's website, where you will be able to see a large selection of photographs taken during this journey, as well as the GPS downloads of our routes.

This Isn't a Travel Guide

There are no fat people in Morocco.

Trust me - I think they passed a law.

Also, I have no doubt that somewhere there's a rule stipulating that only men are permitted to sit on the cheap plastic chairs in dim cafes drinking tea and watching football at full volume.

I'm not sure about these, of course.

But that's the way it *is*.

If you want to find out all the specific facts about the culture and history and architecture and culinary delights offered by this wonderful country, then buy a travel guide.

This isn't a travel guide.

It wasn't meant to be one.

It's a personal account of a motorcycle journey my son and I made to Morocco in March 2013 and it's full of details you won't find in your bog-standard travel guide - the roads and tracks we followed, the adventures we experienced, the people we met along the way, some personal reflections and lots about bikes.

I make no apologies: We ride bikes, we travel on bikes, we *like* bikes so there will be quite a bit in here about motorbikes. It's got a bike on the cover, dammit, so you can't say you were misled.

(If you drive a campervan, air conditioned or otherwise, stop reading this now. It's not for you. You really won't like it - trust me.)

We embarked on the trip with no real, detailed itinerary. That's the way we prefer to travel. It gives you the freedom to do whatever you want to, go where you like without being tied to a pre-determined plan.

The basic idea was this: Ride to Portsmouth, take the ferry to Santander, ride the six hundred miles to Algeciras, take the ferry to Morocco, cross the Atlas Mountains into the Sahara on the other side and see what happens.

And lots happened.

More than we expected - and just what we hoped.

We got stuck in the sand; we got stuck in the snow and fell over in the mud; we teamed up for a few days with a group of mad French outfit riders with their guide in the mountains; we crossed a section of desert with some Belgians in Land Cruisers when our guide dumped us in the middle of nowhere; we began to learn how to ride a loaded bike through soft desert sand and get a feel for navigating through a remote desert region in Southern Morocco.

We ate lots of *tajine*.

We drank very little beer.

We had a ball...

Without doubt, it was a memorable trip and I hope reading this might tempt you to give it a try. At the end I'll include a link that details our route with GPS coordinates and my email address for any questions you might have. Feel free to contact me.

Sir Ranulph Fiennes doesn't complain

We set off in the early-morning darkness, clean, ship-shape and enthusiastic - like schoolboys on an adventure - and the rain pissed down on us for four solid days, just for spite. As we neared Portsmouth a slightly balding man in his late thirties opened the window of his car after pulling up next to us at a set of traffic lights. It was bitterly cold. The sun was not yet properly up, the sky dull and heavily overcast. Frost spiked the grass with white on either side of the road.

"Where you headed?" he called out the window.

I contemplated trying to raise my visor so I could speak more intelligibly but in the end just shouted, "Morocco."

He paused, checking us and the bikes out - like dodgy men on the street do with women - giving us the once-over.

The lights changed.

"Have a good trip!" he called after us as we pulled off.

And it brought to mind a similar experience fifteen years before when my son, Gareth, then just seventeen, and I were riding through Johannesburg in the rain on our old XT500s, weighed down with a 20-litre jerry can, spare tyres, tank bags hand-sewn from old army *bal-sacs* hanging from our petrol tanks; and a man - just like this one - wound down his window whilst driving alongside us and called out, "Where you going?"

And, with a little thrill of pride coming over me, I shouted over the noise of the bikes and the Johannesburg traffic, "England -"

"Good luck!" he shouted after us...

Gareth turned eighteen the day before we crossed the channel and entered England. Now, he's thirty-three and still riding bikes. At least I taught him something worthwhile in life.

Later, on the ferry to Santander, a man walked up to us as we were relaxing in the lounge and said, "We drove behind you quite a bit of the way to the ferry port. Where are you going?"

"Morocco -" I replied again.

He nodded, as if giving it some thought. "Nice -"

What is it about motorcycles packed for travelling that prompts men - and, in my experience, it always has been men - to approach or call out to a total stranger asking about his destination, checking out the bikes with casual flicks of their eyes as if afraid to be caught laying bare their vulnerable yearnings? It's probably the same for the drivers of heavily laden 4X4s (Land Rovers, usually, because of the image) - jerry cans, hi-lift jack and sand mats strapped to the roof rack - heading off into some far-off wilderness.

The answer, I believe, is that deep inside most people is the desire to break free of the mundane predictability of job and home, the monotony of a nine-to-five life, with perhaps some sport over the weekend, a visit to the supermarket for milk, the newspaper and a few beers; and seeing a bike packed for remote travel is a call to adventure that wells up inside and, by approaching someone who *has* managed to break free, talking to them - even just asking, "Where you heading?" - makes them feel, just for a moment, part of the dream. It's the laden big trailie heading along the motorway which sticks in the mind and causes a man to approach you later and say, "We drove behind you..." to lean out of the window of his safe suburban car and call out, "Where you goin'?" because it holds within itself the promise of adventure somewhere down the road.

For me, this trip was special for two reasons:

Firstly, we were headed over the Atlas Mountains and then into the Sahara on the other side to follow a series of *pistes* recommended by Chris Scott, a guy who has explored much of the Sahara by motorcycle; we planned to get as close to the Algerian border as we could without being arrested and possibly do some off-roading across the desert, depending on conditions - accept whatever came in a spirit of un-organised (as distinct from *dis*-organised) travel. The Sahara has always held a fascination for me; a longing to travel across its vast emptiness has always been with me ever since I bought my first Land Rover in 1973 but was prevented from attempting a trans-Africa trip because I was a South African with a white skin. Understandably, most people didn't like us much and didn't really want us travelling in or through their countries. (They didn't want to play rugby or cricket against us either, but that's another story.) I'd crossed a section of the Sahara as part of the Plymouth-Dakar Old Bangers Rally in 2005 but now I was about to attempt it on a bike.

But, secondly, because I was doing the trip with my son. After our trans-Africa trip in 1997 he still loves bikes and his eyes sparkle at the thought of adventure travel. We did a trip to Russia together last year and he is obviously not ashamed to travel again with his ageing parent.

I appreciate that.

I developed a love of adventure travel from my father and am pleased that Gareth has developed some of his desire to explore far-off places from me. It's a rare privilege to know that your child shares with you a similar passion, something that can be experienced together.

And so, as the ferry made its slow way to Spain and we rested in our tiny cabin, we discussed with a delicious sense of anticipation what lay ahead after the six hundred mile traverse of Spain to Algeciras and the crossing to Africa.

At noon the next day we disembarked onto Spanish soil after twenty-four long hours and made our way out of Santander under an overcast sky, the air cold and fresh after the stuffy confines of the ferry.

I'm compelled to admit that we treated the crossing of Spain as little more than a dreary impediment to our adventure in Morocco - six hundred cold and rainy miles to endure. So we put our heads down and rode stoically until it began to get dark. The skies were overcast and threatening rain and we were battered by head and cross winds so strong at times that I was convinced we might be knocked down. The plateau we climbed shortly after leaving Santander was snow-covered and remotely beautiful, as were the Sierra des Gredos that we crossed as evening approached; then the clouds darkened and it began to rain.

And it continued to rain for the next three days.

If you ride a motorbike you will know the universally accepted formula:

$$(motorbike + rain)^3 = unhappy\ biker$$

but, strangely, other than the discomfort and the cold and the wet, it didn't *really* worry us. We were on an adventure! (And I bet Sir Ranulph Fiennes doesn't complain when it rains on *him* - or when his fingers and toes fall off in the snow.)

We reassured each other by insisting that the rain will always stop - sometime - and, anyway, we were headed for the desert and everyone knows it doesn't rain in the desert.

Does it?

As evening approached we found a cheap hotel in the small town of Plasencla, unloaded and secured our bikes then walked (in the rain) into the town centre for a bite to eat. A small café looked promising: warm and dry with hot, fatty smells to pamper our cold bodies. Inside, perched precariously on tall metal bar stools were three very large women. They were eating chips. One would have thought their bulging trousers hanging over the sides of the bar stools would have sent a message: *Fewer chips, more exercise, p-l-e-a-s-e!* - but they obviously weren't listening.

There are no fat people in Morocco.

Typing this up now and thinking back on our trip brings it all back.

There are no fat people in Ethiopia either. That's why they win all the marathons.

Anyway, at that moment, some fatty food was just what Gareth and I needed - and we had obviously come to the right place. The menu offered *BOCATA'S BRUTALES* and we could choose from a *Titanic, Animal, Bestial, Potent, Brutal* or, for the very hungry, a *Potent-Giganitc* .

Brutal food indeed...

Who were we to pass up such tempting treats? The *Potent-Giganitc* sounded just about right, whatever it was. No English was spoken by the dark-eyed Spanish beauty behind the counter so we ordered blind and were served delicious smoky-flavoured rolls filled with bacon and peppers and omelette and various other garlicky things.

To me, this is one of the pleasures of foreign travel - sampling local beers and food from small, noisy cafes whose choice of décor favours white plastic and posters advertising beer and missing cats.

Then back to the hotel where we draped our wet riding gear from curtain rails, window ledges and any other surface or hook that would take them, turned up the heat and vainly hoped they would be dry by the morrow.

They weren't.

Lazy and paranoid border officials

The next day it was still raining. We loaded the bikes on the pavement then grimly set off to ride the three hundred miles across southern Spain to Algeciras through steady, cold rain.

It wasn't particularly pleasant, although the road was good and relatively free of traffic.

Our outer defences had been breached and we were getting increasingly wet. Fortunately my riding trousers (Gortex lining, *nogal)* were proving up to the task - there is little worse than riding all day with cold water pooling around your balls. And although my Gortex socks - best bit of kit I've ever had, trust me - stank the room out at night, they kept my feet dry. Gareth was getting pretty wet but he didn't complain. He never complains. *Stoical* would be a good word to describe him. I'm pleased that he doesn't whinge.

The highlight - if you can call it that - of the day was talking to two British truckers in a café who had seen the RUS stickers on our bikes and asked whether we'd been to Russia. We admitted to having had that pleasure and we settled down to a friendly chin wag - mainly centered around the strange paranoia of Russian officials in positions of authority. These truckers had just returned from Moscow having transported cars there from Britain to take part in some Top Gear event being held by

Jeremy Clarkson and his juvenile gang. We spent the next half hour relating stories about the lobotomised sense of humour and intimidating manner of Russian border officials. It had taken the drivers three hours to get their five trucks into Russia and *seven hours* to get them out again. Evidently the customs officials had found four rolled-up promotional posters and a helmet cam in one truck that had not been declared on the manifest.

This made the Russian customs man angry.

Very angry.

When the trucker tried to placate him by saying, in his most grovelling, ingratiating manner, "It's OK - no problem -" probably crouching a little to show his subservience and spreading his hands in a gesture of surrender, the Russian border official screamed at him,

"It... is... *not...* OK!"

He made a note in the trucker's passport and on the computer and warned him that he would not be welcome back into Russia again.

It reminded me of when we exited Russia last year and I couldn't immediately put my hands on a particular document the stern-faced, unsmiling border official had demanded. Within seconds he began to threaten me with the serious consequences of not being able to produce the document. That flustered me somewhat and I scrabbled helplessly through my file, looking for the document. I knew I had it somewhere because in Russia it's best to keep *every* piece of paper you are given by anyone - just in case. And I had, so it had to be in my file somewhere. I found it in the end, fortunately, or else I might still be locked up in a dark cell somewhere in the Gulag.

Strange people, the Russians. So bitterly filled with suspicion. And yet, we were treated with such friendship and hospitality by the ordinary, rural folk we met.

These truckers had also transported an Aston Martin belonging to the king of Morocco to England and back - for a routine service. The Aston Martin was one of the king's personal fleet of cars. The truckers were delayed from leaving because the king had not yet woken up and could not be disturbed.

They finally got away at noon.

I wonder how many rural Moroccans could be provided with clean running water for the cost of buying and maintaining the king's private fleet of cars?

If Einstein can make up strange-sounding formulae, how about one of mine I've just thought of:

The poverty of the inhabitants of any country shares an inverse relationship with the amount of money wasted on themselves by its self-serving, money-grabbing rulers.

Makes me think of South Africa...

We finally reached Algeciras, tired and slightly damp, made our way to the port and booked tickets for the five pm ferry. It finally left at six thirty - acting, so it seemed, on the African taxi principle of waiting until it was full before setting off.

But I might be wrong; it might have just been late.

The border crossing into Morocco was, as expected, frustrating. In Africa, as in Russia, they don't go out of their way to make it a happy experience to enter or leave their blessed domains. After completing what seemed to be all the required formalities, we were left to stand about at the border for about half an hour. Fortunately it had stopped raining. Three officials wandered aimlessly about, smoking. Finally, one managed to gather the energy to tell us we needed some stamp or other in our passports that only the harbour police section could give. He pointed vaguely in the direction of a far-off building. Very hot in our riding gear, feeling sweaty from the day's ride, we made our way in the general direction of the building only to be pounced upon by a "helper", a "facilitator", who tried to marshal us through the front door. We informed him, politely, that we could cope without his assistance but he hovered about us, insisting that it was "very difficult" and he could help.

We ignored him and, after a while, he got the message and left.

Inside, sadly, we experienced the inimitable joys of dealing with lazy African officials (sorry, do I sound just a tad jaundiced? I've *lived* there. I *know!*) It soon became clear that no one really wanted the hassle of dealing with us. We approached one window and the man wafted a languid hand and muttered, "Upstairs." It was almost too much of an effort to raise his arm sufficiently to point.

We dutifully made our way upstairs.

The man at the upstairs window lazily pointed and said, "Downstairs."

We went downstairs. Well, Gareth "went" - I hobbled. I was overheating in my riding gear and my damaged knee (an unsuccessful wheelie from years back, since you ask) had swollen up and was making it very painful to walk.

Back to the first window.

The same lazy man waved a lethargic hand in the general direction of the ceiling and muttered, "Upstairs."

We remonstrated. We spoke loudly and gesticulated.

He waved us away. "Upstairs -"

At that moment an important looking official wearing a crisply-ironed uniform walked by so we quickly apprehended him before he disappeared through a door, and explained our frustration.

He looked annoyed, directed us to the window we'd just been turned away from and angrily instructed the man to do his job (well, that's what I assume he told him because the official, now wide awake and sitting up straight like a schoolchild when the teacher walks in), took our documents, checked them and stamped a very important number in our passports.

We didn't know this at the time but, without this number, we would have got nowhere in Southern Morocco: at the entrance to and exit from *every* town and village police would check our papers and note down this number.

Anyway, paperwork sorted, we climbed back onto the bikes, found our way out of the harbour (more by luck than design) and set off in the dark to look for somewhere to stay for the night. The heavens opened - again - and we were drenched. The roads quickly became rivers. A high wind had blown over a truck, which partially blocked the road at a roundabout, but on our bikes we were able to squeeze past. We battled on through flooded roads and horizontal rain into Tangier, trying to see through wet and misted visors. Eventually we found a small hotel where, after booking in, we stripped off all our gear and again hung it up all around the room. Perhaps this time it would be dry by morning and we wouldn't have to climb out of a warm bed and pull on clammy, wet gear.

It wasn't.

First puncture and a flooded road

The next day we dragged on our damp clothing (ever tried forcing your hands into sodden gloves?), loaded the bikes in the rain and made our way through a flooded landscape where every turbulent stream and river was stained yellow from run-off. It continued to rain all day as we made our slow way up into the foothills of the Atlas mountains. The soil could hold no more water. Fields had turned into lakes. We passed crowds of people standing on the edges of swollen rivers watching the waters rise; showing more trust in their engineers than I would have, they leaned over bridges that were almost overwhelmed by swirling, muddy water. Obviously this wasn't an everyday event. Riverulets turned into torrents and gushed down mountain slopes until, at times, the road itself became a river as we sloshed our way from the inundated lowlands ever upwards into the mountains.

This was our fourth day of rain and we, especially Gareth whose riding gear seemed to let more water in than it kept out, were damp and smelling of mould. Our hands had taken on that puckered and wrinkled look you get when you spend too much time in the bath. My boots had started to de-laminate and I was beginning to look and smell like someone who sleeps the night under bridges with a friendly dog. In many places the rushing water had undermined the road, causing it to collapse into newly-formed gullies and tumble down the mountainside; these huge bites out of the road were usually, but not always, marked off with boulders so the unwary driver didn't suddenly plunge off a sharp edge and down the side of a mountain. And still the wind howled about us, buffeting us all over the road. We came across another two trucks that had been blown over, their loads scattered into the mud.

But we were happy.

Damp and cold, but happy.

The built-up lowlands were behind us at last and we were steadily making our way into more remote regions through the foothills of the Rif Rif mountains towards Chefchaouen; the riding conditions were challenging and, therefore, exciting.

We felt as if, at last, our adventure had started.

The familiar characteristics of rural, high Morocco that I remembered so clearly from the Plymouth-Dakar Old Bangers Rally began to emerge from the rain and mist which shrouded the mountains: avenues of gum trees, their smooth white trunks standing out against the dark leaves and rain blackened rocks; laden donkeys standing with patient stoicism on the sides of the road; olive green cacti, their outermost leaves bearing fruit which hung like blood clots on their thick, leathery edges; unpainted mud and concrete houses blended into the sodden landscape. Children waved to us as we passed through small villages. Trucks, so heavily laden with bales of hay that their front wheels seemed on the point of lifting off the road, made their slow, ponderous way up the sides of mountains, slowing us down. The many tight curves, the narrow, pot-holed roads and the rain made passing difficult.

By late morning we had crossed the Rif Rif mountains and immediately were riding under a deep blue sky, warm and bright. To the east, rain clouds hung darkly over the mountaintops as we made our slow, winding way towards Chefchaouen, a blue town perched high up in the mountains.

One of the most beautiful aspects of many Moroccan cities is the wash they use to paint their houses. Whether this is determined by the soil found locally that is used as a wash over the walls and which differs from one location to the next, or whether a decision is made by local elders about the colour houses can be painted, I am not sure (look it up in your handy travel guide) but the houses in many towns tend to be painted in one shade - Fes, for example, is predominantly blue, Meknes green, Rabat white, Marrakesh red. As we approached Chefchaouen through a rain-darkened landscape, the pale shades of blue - those houses not painted this delicate dove's-egg blue were painted white - created a calm, restful feeling about this pretty town that clings with an ageless tenacity to the sodden mountainside.

Then it started to rain again.

We filled up with petrol and made our way south towards Ouazzane, deciding to follow a small road that wound its way through remote mountain valleys for a hundred miles towards Fes. Taking smaller roads usually proves more interesting, leading the traveller into more remote parts of a country where you can feel the bones of the land beneath your tyres. But those one hundred miles took us six hours to complete. We could only do about twenty miles an hour at best through the increasingly pot-holed, sodden road that snaked its way up and down mountainsides and alongside flooded rivers.

We stopped for lunch at a tiny shop/cafe with cheap plastic chairs and wood chips covering the floor. A group of men and boys stared at us and the bikes from the road outside. As usual, there were no women. The men were helpful; the coffee was strong and hot. And at least we were out of the rain for a while.

Then, in the early afternoon, Gareth pulled over with a punctured rear tyre. So much for Ultraseal. On the box they assure you that the intelligent little fibres will worm their way into any hole and block it - but I've never yet found a tyre sealant that works. All they usually do is make the tube so mucky you can't get a patch to stick when you give up on the little fibres miraculously doing their silent work. But, to be fair, I don't think Ultraseal is really intended for use on tubed tyres; and I personally have never had a puncture whilst using Ultraseal - but then you can't prove a negative. Maybe I've just not ridden over any thorns or bits of metal yet. (I put all this in so I don't get sued by Ultraseal's highly paid lawyers.)

We pumped up the tyre in the rain (using my newly-purchased *Slime* electric pump - best bit of kit I've bought after the Gortex socks - and I hope they send me lots of money for this endorsement) and rode on. But after a few miles the tyre was flat again. We pulled onto the verandah of what looked like a deserted house to get out of the driving rain, unloaded the bikes, removed the wheel and replaced the tube.

A brief pause for some "Essential Kit to take on Bike Rides" advice. If you're the kind of biker who can rebuild your gearbox on the side of the road with a shifting spanner and a bent screwdriver, skip this paragraph.

Both Gareth and I carried a spare front and rear tube as well as puncture repair kits. If there's one thing other than major engine failure or running out of petrol that will cause you serious angst in the middle of the desert, it is flat tyres. Other than the *Slime* pump, Gareth had invested in a set of good quality tyre irons specially designed for motorcycle rims. (If you've ever tried to remove a rear tyre with those Mickey-mouse little six-inch things they give you in your standard tool kit, you'll know what I'm talking about.) And pumping up tyres by hand in the middle of desert heat is really not recommended. Trust me, if you're contemplating a trip where you will not be able to summon those friendly men who help little old ladies on the side of the road and who load your bike onto the back of a truck and take it to a garage where efficient men in overalls whip your tyre off, replace the tube (it seems no one repairs punctures any more) and ease it back on again with copious slatherings of soap while you drink coffee and look at magazines full of voluptuous ladies draped over the bonnets of cars, do yourself a favour and buy a good quality, compact electric pump and a set of decent (at least 300mm long) tyre irons. When you are sitting in the hot sand one day with your belongings spread about the desert replacing a tube, you'll bless me for this advice. And just one more thing: if you struggle to break the bead, use your side stand and the weight of the bike to press it off the rim. It works a treat.

Tube replaced, we rode on in the rain, the offending sliver of metal - almost like the pocket clip on a fountain pen - tucked away as a memento.

By five the rain stopped for a blessed hour, the road dried out and Gareth and I rode hard along an exciting switchback of a road, steep gradients with sharp bends as we made our way over a succession of mountain ranges. We pushed our riding close to the edge of safety, revelling in the tyres' grip on a dry road after days of rain, trying to reach Fes before darkness overtook us. All about us were flooded fields, rivers breaking their banks and rushing across the road in muddy swathes.

Then we rounded a bend to be met with a number of cars and trucks stopped and backed up. The road was blocked.

We pulled up to see that a section of road about fifty metres wide was flooded, the water running smooth and deep enough to deter these drivers. It didn't look impassable so I got off my bike and gingerly walked into the water, stepping carefully in case I disappeared into a deep hole like some of the sections of washed-away road we had come across in the mountains. In just one place it was fairly deep - up to the middle of my calf - and running strongly but I felt it was do-able so walked back and sent Gareth across first. (That's what sons are for, isn't it? If he got washed away then I'd know it wasn't safe to cross and look for an alternative way round.) He made it fairly easily, and then it was my turn. In the deep section the water tugged and pushed against the wheels and engine a little but it wasn't a problem.

The drivers, who had been watching us as if we were mad, clapped and patted us on the back as soon as we had made it across, then they started driving through themselves. They probably got home and said something like, "Hi, honey, I'm home! Sorry I'm late - road somewhat flooded. We waited until two stupid Englishmen on motorbikes rode across. When they weren't washed away and drowned we knew it was safe. Fortunately there's always some idiot who will be the first to try to get across a flooded road."

As darkness began to fall, rain came down again, hard this time and we had to slow right down, especially when the road rose into the mist, cutting visibility down to about ten metres.

Finally, after seven, we finally saw the lights of Fes far below us in a valley; it took us a while to make our way down in the rain and dark, the road winding its way with numerous tight bends. As we entered the town, a car pulled up in front of us and a most helpful man offered to lead us to a cheap hotel. He claimed to have no personal interest in the deal, said he worked for the Moroccan tourist industry - and so he might have but, the next day, we found that we were charged double what he had said the hotel would cost.

This was our first experience of the slickly-efficient, Moroccan-wide system of getting hold of tourists *before* they enter a town and leading them to a hotel, restaurant, garage, souvenir shop, whatever, owned by a "friend". The networking system functions with seamless efficiency. It must work on a *quid pro quo* basis or perhaps small commissions are paid; in the end, though, we found it more than tiring and tended to ignore the shouted invitations to a *tête-à-tête* by men usually dressed in brightly coloured *djellaba* so you can't miss them.

As soon as we were in the hotel, this guy tried to get us to book a tour into the desert with a guide, all the bells and whistles. We declined, wanting our desert experience to be a personal one and not mediated by *faux* guides wearing traditional costume to impress the tourists.

But, despite this, our hotel room was warm and dry, we were provided with a lock-up garage for the bikes, our wet clothes were soon decorating the room and dripping sadly on the floor and we were seated at a low table eating our first *tajine*. No beer, sadly, in this strictly Islamic country (although we learned later from more experienced Moroccan travellers that, as the Americans found during prohibition, there is always a back door; rather expensive, but always there).

Oasis camp and the attentions of Abdel

When we woke the next day, the sun had finally decided to get its act together. After four days of rain, it was like balm for tortured souls; we stood in the street outside the hotel, faces uplifted, absorbing the rays like new-age sun-worshippers. I had to restrain myself from lifting my hands heavenwards and crying "Hallelujah!"

We pulled on our still-damp clothes, squished our feet into sodden and slowly disintegrating boots, loaded the bikes and set off heading south for Azrou, Ar-Rachidia and, hopefully, the desert. The road was good and we climbed steadily to two thousand metres up the Massif du Kandar, a desolate, wind-swept plateau with pockets of snow wherever direct sunlight could not reach. All day the wind buffeted us from the west; when I was behind Gareth, it was most comical to see him riding straight yet with a pronounced lean against the prevailing wind as if he was leaning into a tight turn. In the distance the dark, snow-capped barrier of the Haut Atlas stretched right across the horizon, seeming to bar our way to the east.

After crossing this high desolate plateau, we descended to fifteen hundred metres and rode across the aptly named Plateau de Arid, a flat, rocky, semi-desert landscape inhabited only by a few shepherds tending their flocks which somehow manage to survive by cropping the sparse tufts of coarse grass that cling to life between the rocks. And still the wind pressed coldly against us from a lowering sky. As we neared the foothills, the Haut Atlas range seemed to grow in height, an impenetrable rock wall, blue-black and snow-capped, rising straight out of the semi-desert floor, a starkly impressive sight. But before we actually began to climb, the road suddenly turned east and we rode parallel to the mountains for about twenty miles before entering them through the Gorges Duiziz, a series of steep-sided valleys that made their way over and through the mountains. As we climbed, the landscape quickly changed to a rocky desert where nothing grew except in the sandy bed of shallow rivers, flowing strongly after the heavy rains in the mountains over the past week. Then the occasional date palm began to appear, especially around Ar-Rachidia, an impressive town in the middle of nowhere, set amongst large date plantations which are irrigated from a dam we passed further to the north.

About five kilometres past Ar-Rachidia we came across a delightful campsite set in an oasis amongst tall palms watered from natural springs that emerge from under the rocks and flow through a series of well-constructed canals. The oasis is almost hidden, below the natural level of the ground and is easy to miss. One turns off the road that makes its seemingly endless, straight way across a rocky desert landscape, the road dips between vertical rocky walls and there, in the middle of this starkly dead landscape, is a hidden valley of green, waving palm trees and small plots of cultivated land irrigated by the channelled water. In the campsite one is surrounded by the sounds of running water, birdcalls and the quiet rustling of palm leaves.

While Gareth rode back to town to buy some oil, I took a long walk up the palm-covered gorge until I found where the water gushed from the side of a cliff. I crouched and drank its sweet coolness, cupping it in my hands.

I was alone; the whole world was silent.

I paused for a while to reflect and absorb my surroundings: some thirty foot above me, the desert stretched away to the east, across the Sahara for thousands of miles. The groundwater I had just drunk might have lain deep under the rocks and sand for millions of years...

On the way back I came across a woman and child who had been collecting dry palm fronds for firewood. They had loaded these onto the back of a small donkey, packed and tied them so high that very little of the donkey was still visible. Not content with that, both the woman and child had managed to climb up and ensconce themselves on top of the pile, balanced precariously on the donkey's back. The woman had dropped a plastic bottle of water and was trying to pick it up by thrusting a stick through the handle - without success. I watched for a while, unobserved, this ancient tableau that dated back before the time of Christ. All the while the donkey stood patiently, its thin legs splayed for balance. And once again I was saddened at the way, throughout the world, the patient, stoical donkey is abused, a beast of burden so unfeelingly treated. Throughout our time in Morocco we were to see these small animals being forced to carry impossibly heavy loads and, instead of walking alongside or leading the poor beast, the owners would climb on top, adding their weight to the already heavily burdened animal. I realise I am looking at this through the eyes of a Westerner, my bleeding heart quivering in my critical breast, and I should see the donkey through the eyes of poor people for whom the creature is as utilitarian as a pick-up truck, tractor, wheel barrow - but I just wish they would show a little more compassion.

I left the woman still trying to hook her water bottle with a stick and made my way back to the campsite through the gathering darkness only to find that some very hungry and persistent cats had managed to chew a hole through the strong nylon bag I used to carry our supplies and were happily gnawing their way into a large salami I had brought along for emergencies. They were, understandably, most reluctant to leave. I relieved them of their half-finished meal, took out my penknife and cut off the chewed bits, feeding them to the hovering cats, and stowed what was left in a more secure place.

Later we met Abdel, a community elder who helped run the campsite. He invited us to share some "Berber whisky" with him and his son. We looked puzzled.

"Tea!" he laughed, pleased with his little joke.

He led us into a cool, dark room and sat us down on low, softly-cushioned chairs, the floor covered with carpets. It is interesting how these desert people have discovered how to keep the inside of their dwellings cool in the heat of the desert. Thick adobe walls, small, shuttered windows for light, walls covered in colourful tiles insulate the houses from the heat outside. There were many times on the trip when we were invited out of the desert heat to find ourselves in a cool, darkened room lavishly carpeted and decorated, where we could strip off our jackets and relax in the comfort of soft, low settees and drink something cool. It was somehow surreal, like stepping into another world.

Abdel, while pouring our sweet, black tea into small bowls in the traditional way, lifting the aluminium teapot high in the air and allowing the stream of liquid to fall into the bowls without a drop being spilled, told us that the campsite and surrounding lands are jointly owned by the community. I asked him about a huge ruin of a building which looked like the remains of a fort, built of adobe and slowly being absorbed back into the soil that I had seen on the opposite cliff-top of the gorge when I went for my walk. He told us it was the remains of the village Kasbah that they had abandoned sixty years ago. He didn't say why.

When we had finished our tea, he offered to cook us our evening meal. Having experienced this kind of offer before and knowing it to be a clever ploy, the main aim of which is to transfer money from our pocket to his, I asked him how much he would charge.

"Anything you like to give!" he said, smiling, opening his arms wide as if he was about to hug us both. "When you are happy, I am happy!" he added.

I must admit I was suspicious of Abdel and his gentle-eyed son, Mohammed. When travelling through a foreign country, one wants to get to know the real people living their real lives, not those putting on a charade for the tourists, pseudo individuals out for a quick buck. I want to experience the food they eat, the music they listen to, the homes they live in - not the food they think tourists would like (one gets *so* tired of the endless offer of *tajine*), not the set display of local musicians dressed in local garb playing for a bunch of glassy-eyed tourists who are then encouraged to dance in an embarrassed and reluctant way. I always try to get as far away from places tourists visit when travelling in a foreign country because it is only then that you can be sure you are meeting ordinary people going about their ordinary lives rather than seeing that which has been dressed up as a tourist display.

And Abdel seemed so genuine in his offer of tea and a meal, so interested in sharing something about his way of life to us, answering our questions and being sociable.

But I was on my guard. I wondered when he would put the pressure on, bring out his store of shiny baubles especially made for the tourist trade. Or ask us to sign a visitor's book with a column for "Donations" to help cover the hospital fees for an illusory ill child as we had experienced in Ethiopia, the many subtle tricks played so expertly by cynical touts who have become skilled in removing money from unwary or gullible tourists. Even though we'd been in the country for a very short time, already we were tired of the false approaches offering friendship as we entered towns or villages, smiling young men (it is always the men) filled with a pseudo bonhomie,

"Hello, my friend! How are you?"

A warm shaking of the hand which one finds difficult to refuse - *not* to shake a proffered hand would be taken as a sign of rudeness, of rejection, even of racism or condescension - so one takes the hand. Now a bond has been formed and it is difficult just to walk away, to ignore the personable young man who sticks to you like a leech offering advice, assistance, asking personal questions:

"Where are you from? London? Ah, Manchester! Manchester City! Football! I have a friend who lives in London. What is your name? You want something to eat? Some *tajine?* You want a hotel?"

Or, if they are selling something, after the warm handshake and the friendly questions, you become aware of the sly look that comes into the eyes, a conspiratorial tone in the voice like someone selling dirty postcards, and some piece of tourist tat is unwrapped from a dirty cloth, semi-precious stones, or fossils, silver bracelets perhaps, an invitation to come into a nearby shop.

"No, we're on motorbikes, we don't want to buy anything."

"Just look - you don't have to buy."

"No, we don't want anything."

"You want to eat? Some *tajine?*"

"No, thank you, no *tajine.*"

"You want desert experience. Sleep in a tent. Go by camel?"

"No, we are heading into the desert on our own, thank you."

"You want a hotel?"

And so it goes on, endlessly. One doesn't want to be rude, that would be churlish; after all, they are just trying to make a living, but it becomes so tiring, so predictable, so annoying one longs to get away, out into the wide open spaces of nothingness where the camper vans don't go, where the tourist rot hasn't yet begun to fester and suppurate.

One is flagged down at the entrance to towns; they wait for you, step into the road, call out to you to stop. At first we did, assuming there was something important we needed to know, or perhaps they needed our assistance, but we soon learned to ignore them, to drive by looking for a café that locals would eat in, a hotel in a backwater street that no self-respecting tourist would think of entering.

But it didn't happen. We enjoyed our meal. Abdel played a little joke, at first giving us just bread with a plate of tomato and onion, implying that this was our meal. Then, laughing, he brought out the *tajine* followed by oranges and coffee. It was delicious and, on the surface, it seemed as if he was doing it just for us, because he liked us, because he wanted to be our friends. But it was tiring having him there all the time, talking, always talking. After a long day riding under the hot sun, sometimes you just want to sit in quiet, companionable silence, savour the atmosphere, make a brief comment about something that happened during the day. But always Abdel was there, talking.

And, ever so slowly, we realised what he was doing: Carefully he steered the conversation towards the "desert experience", telling us about the trips he had taken tourists on - "One or two days, a week if you want, sleep the night in a Tuareg tent in the dunes, authentic food. Look -" he said, pulling out his mobile phone and showing us videos of tourists climbing onto camels, tourists dancing with embarrassed determination to "authentic" local musicians in traditional dress beating drums as part of his "Desert Experience". He suggested it might be a bad idea for us to go into the desert on our own; the sand would be too soft for our bikes, he assured us, with all the rain, the *oeds* would be high and we would have difficulty crossing them... "- better you leave your motorbikes, put your luggage on my 4X4 and I will arrange to take you into the desert, sleep in the dunes for one day, maybe two, sleep in a tent, wake up to traditional Berber breakfast then my 4X4 will bring you back to your motorbikes. Much easier this way."

No, we wanted to go on our own. We wanted to camp in the desert by ourselves. No, we didn't want a pre-packed experience. No, we wouldn't like to dance as the sun set across the dunes.

To give him his due, he accepted this, didn't press further but asked whether we were calling in at Marrakesh - "I have a friend who owns a hotel in Marrakesh. He will give you a good price..."

Networking, always networking. Everyone has a friend who owns a garage, a hotel, a camel, a restaurant. And we came to realise that, really, the invitation to the meal was just to give him an opportunity to promote his "Desert Experience", to have us buy the meal from him rather than prepare something for ourselves.

And the price of our supper? I realised that that too was carefully calculated. "Pay what you want! I am happy if you are happy!" Well, it would be a churlish person indeed who did not make a generous payment for such personal attention, such hospitality. In fact, I would imagine most tourists who are given the full and undivided attention of Abdul - the welcome tea, the interesting anecdotes, the little joke about *Berber Whiskey* - would end up paying more than what would normally be asked for at a restaurant because not to do so would be insulting, a rejection of the *friendship* so freely offered.

I must admit I was confused. Were we being very carefully manipulated by an astute businessman or was Abdul genuinely interested in us as people - and slipping in a little salesmanship along the way?

Perhaps a bit of both.

As we left, he insisted we join him for a cup of tea before we left next morning.

We decided not to.

Plastic Jesus

But, the next morning, after waking to the lugubrious cooing of doves in the palms above us, we packed up and headed towards the exit, only to be met by an anxious Mohammed telling us that our tea was ready and had been prepared for us.

How could we refuse?

The desert was calling loudly and insistently - but it would be unmannerly to refuse. We reluctantly left the bikes and made our way back into the cool, shady room with the gentle-eyed Mohammed who turned out to be his father's son, only less subtle. He immediately started talking, informing us that, as a good Moslem, he watched no TV - "The stars are my TV!" he cooed, waving his arm to express the vastness of space - and I wondered cynically how many times he had said this to gullible tourists. He poured our tea, talking, ever talking, just like his father; then, with the sleight of hand worthy of a conjurer, a cotton bag filled with poorly made silver bangles appeared. He pointed out the Berber motifs of camel and tent and suggested we might like to buy one for those at home.

"No, we don't want to buy anything," we assured him.

Undeterred, he took out another, carved with a Southern Cross motif. He proceeded to tell us how Berbers used the stars, and particularly the Southern Cross, to navigate across the endless wastes of the desert. How would we like to buy a bangle with the Southern Cross on it for those loved ones waiting at home?

"No, thank you, we don't want to buy anything," we assured him, the desert outside calling to us with increasing insistence.

"What about a necklace? Or some crystals?"

And as we finally managed to finish our tea and got up to leave, I thought to myself how far from the true desert Tuareg Berber young Mohammed and his father were. They were businessmen, using their proud traditions to sell tourist tat; their Desert Experience is as far from the real thing as a plastic Jesus with flashing neon bleeding heart is to the carpenter with dirt under his nails and sawdust in his hair; about as real as putting the plastic Jesus on your mantelpiece and hoping it will save your soul.

I realise that I have written at length about Abdul and Mohammed here, about being manipulated by wily men looking for a quick buck. At times, my voice has become a little shrill, I fear. But the reason I have dwelt on this at such length is that, in a way, it is central to the ethos of our travelling. When Gareth and I travelled into Russia and were arrested for entering a restricted zone in some *tigian* wilderness, the policeman who was questioning us asked, "Why don't you go to Moscow or St Petersburg like normal tourists?" (He didn't actually say the "like normal tourists" bit - but that was implied.) And we tried to explain to him that we wanted to visit those parts of Russia that the tourists *didn't* visit, see the country in its raw beauty alone and unsupervised, and it was because of this that we had stumbled into a remote restricted zone and been arrested. I think he understood. Just the same, in this country, we didn't want to experience the Morocco neatly packaged for tourists, just as, in a recent flight to South Africa, my wife and I were reluctant to take the two-hour packaged trip by mini-bus to the pyramids to fill a long stop-over in Cairo a year or so back, but we did - and endured a young guide rattling off a potted history of the pharaohs that any schoolboy would know, before leading us to a "friend" who sold over-priced perfume. We peered at the plastic Jesus pyramids from behind a metal fence, feeling gullible and let down, before spending a frustrating hour being emotionally manipulated by a smooth-tongued salesman into buying perfume. Gareth and I, in Morocco, wanted to feel the sand in our hair, the heat of the sun on our backs, smell the smoke of fires preparing food, travel *through* the country rather than passing *over* it in air-conditioned comfort to be met at the entrance to towns by gaily garbed men offering a neatly-wrapped *faux* experience.

The Jesus we wanted to meet in Morocco would have blood on his hands and the marks of thorns in his head...

We dip a toe into the desert

Motorbikes are not really designed to travel across deep, soft sand.

Heavily laden bikes are *definitely* not intended, in the normal course of things, to travel across deep, soft sand.

Gareth and I always knew that.

We had it confirmed this day...

I write this in a wind-blown, sandy tent pitched on the stone-covered slope of a *massif* in the desert about eighteen miles west of the Algerian border. A lone acacia tree, gnarled and weather-beaten, stands next to the tents, giving the illusion of shade. Into the distance in front of us stretches a vast, flat, dry river valley, wind-blown and bare. The sun is low on the horizon, the air beginning to cool.

We are tired to the depths of our bones but deeply satisfied with both the bikes and our achievement. There were times during the day when we wondered just how much more we could take...

We left our shady oasis camp after finally prizing ourselves away from the gently insistent but disappointed Mohammed and his silver bangles, and took to the tourist trail to Merzouga. The road was well maintained and pleasant, mostly following the *Oed* Rheris, which, after the abundant rains in the highlands, was flowing strongly. Where there is water there is life and for mile upon mile the riverbed was thickly planted with date palms. Not being stupid, the local population also gravitate towards water, and we rode through numerous towns and villages tucked in amongst the palms. Because of the abundance of water in the river, they had been irrigating their fields, many of which were flooded between the low sand ridges that separated them and prevented the water spilling out into the desert sand.

This was the main road to Merzouga, jumping off point for the thousands of tourists in camper vans eager to get their taste of the Desert Experience; at the entrance to every town the roadside was cluttered with billboards advertising hotels and restaurants, tour companies offering 4X4 trips into the dunes, quad bike hire, camel rides, nights camped in the dunes etc etc, spoiling the remoteness one looks for in the desert.

Just to the east of Merzouga lies the Erg Chebbi, a small sand sea with beautifully formed dunes, the classic shape one sees in glossy brochures with silhouetted camels and sultry-eyed nomadic beauties inviting you silently to participate in the pleasures of the harem. The gently curving dunes, impressively high against a clear, dark-blue sky, looked invitingly soft, pale brown and smooth. It is no wonder that tourists flock to this place. A good tar road leads one to a modern town full of luxurious hotels and *tajine*-selling restaurants, companies vying with each other to whisk you a short way into the dunes where you can sleep in your Berber tent and eat an authentic Berber breakfast.

I must admit both Gareth and I were eager to get a feel of the real desert sand between our toes (and under the wheels of the bikes). We had stopped so that we could look at the dunes, lying about a mile away from the road, tantalisingly close. With the engines switched off, the land about us was totally still, the empty sky huge above us. We looked at each other, nodded, grinned and headed off road across a firm, flat plain covered with a light dusting of small stones (called *reg*), making straight towards the dunes. We were like children released into a playground after being confined to the house during a long illness. We couldn't wait to play in the sand. Dunes have the delicate curves of an ocean wave, the angles of their slopes precisely dictated by principles of gravity and friction, shaped by insistent pressures of the wind. We wanted to ride across their perfect faces with the same desire as a skier lusts after virgin *pistes*.

At last we were here, so close we could almost touch the smallish, perfectly formed dunes, foothills of the huge accumulations of sand that blocked half the horizon to the east. *This* is what we had come for. This is what we had thought about for many long days riding through the rain. Finally, we had reached the desert...

Gareth reached the dune first. He gleefully accelerated onto the sand.

And got stuck.

Very stuck.

He'd only managed to ride about *five metres* before burying his back wheel. When he got off, the bike remained standing on it own, deeply buried. Then it fell over.

It took both of us to drag the heavy bike out of the sand. Already we were hot and exhausted. What were we *thinking?* How were we going to ride our bikes across sand like this for miles (and we hadn't even loaded up with extra fuel and water yet) when we got stuck within metres of hitting the soft stuff? Maybe the "Desert Experience", clean and sanitised, sitting in a comfortable 4X4 being driven by someone who knows the area to a pretty tent pitched in the dunes and served with cups of sweet tea while we watch the sun set golden across the gentle curves of the sand, like infantile limbs, would not be such a bad idea after all.

Enjoying the moment, I took photos of Gareth and his stuck bike. He took it in good spirit. Then, somewhat chastened, we made our way back to the road. I wimped out and didn't even attempt the sand. It scared me.

We finally reached Merzouga at mid-day, managed to elude all the touts and escape being run over by a thousand camper vans driven by old retired people. (Mental check: *I'm an old retired person.*) Filled with a delicious sense of anticipation as we were about to set off on our first *piste,* we had something to eat then topped up our fuel, filled our water containers and headed out of town...

A brief diversion - Fuel and Water

A brief diversion for those interested (if you don't want to know the petrol and water details, skip on):

We had looked at some of the *pistes* recommended by Chris Scott and, although some of them are relatively short, others are well in excess of our bikes' maximum range; added to this, when we looked at the map, there were interesting small roads across the almost blank southern section of the desert near the Mauritanian border which looked enticing but were very long. If we wanted to do something out of the ordinary, we would have to carry extra fuel and water. Added to that, as we had never travelled across the desert before, we had no idea how riding in soft sand would affect the bikes' fuel consumption. Gareth decided to buy one of those fairly new seven-litre square, flat containers (Rotopax, I think they're called) that he strapped on the seat behind him under his dry-bag; having a smaller tank (fourteen-litres on my KLE500), I opted for two five-litre cheepo petrol containers. To keep the weight low, I devised a somewhat Heath Robinson-ish method of strapping them to the frame just behind the heels of my boots where a pillion passenger's feet would go. This worked well, although I knew they were vulnerable in a crash. In actual fact, with the added cushion of my soft luggage, they took the many falls I had in the sand, mud and on the road well, without splitting or leaking. Far better would be to look for a larger, after-market tank - twenty litres or so - that would give a pretty good range.

Water: we both took four litres, carried as low as possible in our panniers. This, added to our tools, spare tubes, tent and related camping gear, basic foodstuffs, a few spare clothes and odds and sods made us pretty heavy. Many were the discussions we had on how to reduce weight. You *have* to carry food, water, petrol, tools and basic spares. It would be foolhardy to venture into the desert without these. Unless you want to be stupidly macho, you need a sleeping bag. What we decided, in the end, was that we would consider, next time, not bringing a tent or any cooking equipment, sleeping under the stars and bringing food that could be eaten out of a tin or packet. Also, a good idea would be to leave all our warm, wet-weather gear (which we needed for the long ride across Spain and the Atlas Mountains) at a friendly garage or hotel and come back for them later.

As anyone who has ridden long distance on a motorbike over rough terrain knows, it's all about weight and its distribution on the bike. I always feel that if you can't pick your bike up on your own, loaded, then you're probably carrying too much. Get a lighter bike, carry less luggage or spend more time at the gym, you lazy git.

Personally, I would never attempt the *pistes* we did alone. If you can't progress forward (like if you're half way up a soft dune) a heavy bike up to its belly in deep sand is almost impossible to turn round without help. The only way you can do it is to unload the bike, lie it on its side and drag it round by the front wheel. Gareth, strong young man that he is, could lift his bike, loaded, fairly easily; I could just manage to lift mine, putting a great deal of strain on my body, so long as I didn't have to lift it against a slope. That is why keeping the weight as low as possible is paramount; it also helps keeping the bike stable in mud or soft sand. I will never forget trying to work out how to store our luggage on the XT500s for our trans-Africa trip many years ago. I had made light metal carriers above the front headlights of the XTs and thought they were ideal for carrying five-litre water containers. We filled them up, strapped them onto the carriers with bungees and tried to ride the bikes around the house - just as a trial. All the bikes wanted to do was fall over. The weight of five-litres of water in front of the handlebars and above the headlights made them totally unstable. We strapped our sleeping bags there instead and it worked well.

Our first desert piste

So, loaded up and ready, Gareth checked on his GPS and found the track, and we headed out of town, the bikes feeling sluggish and heavy, rolling slightly and slow to respond. Gareth lost his way briefly but felt that he could follow another track on the outskirts of town and rejoin the *piste* a little further on. He was about thirty metres ahead of me. The track crested a rise, the sand turned a reddish orange and Gareth ploughed to a stop half way up, his wheels again deeply buried in the sand. I stopped on the hard ground before the rise and went to help him. There was no way he could get the bike to the top of the low hill as it was and he couldn't budge it backwards. A Spanish man travelling through Morocco in a car had also attempted this hill and got stuck; he, with the help of some locals, had managed to extricate his car and he came over to help us. Together, the three of us pulled the heavy KTM backwards out of the sand and onto hard ground again.

On the getting stuck front, I was winning 2-0. But then, I hadn't ridden in soft sand yet; and if I'd been in front up that small hill, it would have been me trying to push my bike backwards out of the sand and not Gareth.

Interesting, we found on the trip that my smaller KLE was much better in the sand than Gareth's KTM; my five hundred ccs gave me just enough power even in the very soft stuff (although I did have to ride my clutch briefly sometimes to keep up the revs) and the Kawasaki seemed to travel *over* the sand more easily than the KTM, which tended to dig in suddenly and stop, showing a perverse desire to throw Gareth over the handlebars.

So, our second brush with sand and yet again we had very quickly got stuck. The heavily laden bikes were very difficult to move once deeply buried and, in places, definitely needed more than one person to extricate. Had we bitten off more than we could chew here? Already stuck and we hadn't even left the outskirts of the town.

It was a sobering lesson and added to our uncertainty about the wisdom of what we were attempting.

After extricating Gareth's bike, we found the correct track and set off on one of the most difficult and memorable rides I have ever done.

At first the track was easy. Dust- and heat-haze obscured the last buildings of Merzouga behind us; the beautiful, chocolate-box dunes of the Erg Chebbi disappeared below the horizon and were replaced by a desolate landscape of sand and rock. And, suddenly, a sense of release, of freedom came over me. This is what we had come so far to experience. At last we were nudging our way into the desert, devoid of people, camper vans, advertising hoardings, local men dressed in gaily-coloured *djebella* calling, "Hello, my friend ..."

We passed large sections of desert where rows of palm trees had been planted and crude barriers erected in a vain attempt to halt the migration of the dunes. As I rode past these puny constructions, a picture of King Canute came to mind. Nothing is going to stop dunes migrating once the fierce Harmattan begins to blow, lifting the sand grain by grain until the air is turned to milk and visibility is reduced to a few yards.

The ground was firm beneath the wheels, slightly stony with occasional corrugations. In the distance on both sides of us, low ranges of hills, rocky and black, seemed to channel us along through a broken land. The *piste*, a stony dirt track, twisted and undulated around and over small hills, dipped to cross wide, flat river beds; the land was starkly desolate but still the occasional tamarisk tree gave perspective to a dry sameness which stretched to the horizon. We rode standing up most of the time, feeling the bikes responsive under our feet, the extra weight no longer really noticed. There were no sand drifts, no dunes and we made good progress. In fact, all about there was *nothing* except for the desert and the thorn trees and us, making our slow way along tracks that, as the afternoon progressed, became increasingly smaller and more indistinct across the barren landscape. Every so often the *piste* would split and branch, usually where the terrain was rough or very rocky and cars had decided to find their own way. Gareth kept an eye on his GPS (mine had given up through this stretch) and, where tracks of equal size diverged, would point left or right to keep us heading in approximately the right direction.

What we hadn't realised - and were to learn as we explored deeper into the remoter sections of the desert over the next two weeks - is that there is no *single* track, even though on the map it might be shown as such. *Pistes* are formed over time when people travel - usually by car or truck - from one town or village in the desert to another. The first car through leaves its tyre marks in the sand. Others follow. Over the years, decades, the tracks become slight depressions in the sand or rocks and a *piste* is formed. But throughout the decades of formation, cars and trucks leave the main track for whatever reason - to camp for the night, to investigate an interesting feature, to look for water, to find an easier route around soft sand or a rocky outcrop, to get around the migrating tongue of a dune. Later, someone else follows that track... and then someone else. So, instead of a single road, as one would have if it were tar, one is sometimes faced with a filigree of tracks, some more pronounced than others, spreading out over a desolate landscape, joining and re-separating endlessly. For those who know the land, who are able to recognise a mountain range or pronounced landmark in the distance, it is usually not a problem. But for novices, crossing an unknown and uninhabited stretch of desert for the first time, it was somewhat disconcerting. We would certainly have turned back without Gareth's GPS which, although it too, on maximum zoom, showed a maze of tracks, at least we knew we were heading in vaguely the right direction. We would have been completely lost without it.

At last we came across a Moroccan man on a motorbike; we stopped to speak to him and, although it was difficult for us to understand each other, he seemed to be warning us about a river crossing some twenty miles or so ahead. There was nothing we could do about it so we pressed on, no longer quite sure that we were doing the right thing or heading in the right direction.

As the afternoon progressed we began to come across dunes again; on either side of us were long lines of low mountains - buttes where the hard rock cap had not been worn away, rounded where it had. They were particularly beautiful in that the sand was a deep red-brown colour whereas the rock was black, creating scree slopes of deep black overlaying the brown. As the miles fell away, the sand altered colour: grey, yellow, red, brown - and always the overlay of black rocks providing contrast. Then the track descended onto a flat, firm salt pan extending to the horizon and we sped up, loving the smoothness of it, the rush of cool air against our faces.

Then we began to encounter soft sand.

At first it was just short, isolated sections that we could cross with a burst of speed. But, progressively, the deep sand became the norm rather than the exception and we started to struggle.

The problem was this: the softer the sand, the deeper below the surface of the surrounding land the *piste* becomes. The soft edges can be over a foot higher than the wheel ruts through the sand, the *middlemnannetjie* - the sand hump between the wheel tracks - pronounced and very soft. Only later, as we began to learn, did we realise it was far better when encountering belts of this soft sand - what the locals call *fetch fetch* - to leave the track altogether and pick your way across the desert floor on the patches of harder ground. But once you are in the deep, soft, wheel channels it is very difficult to get out; turn the front wheel and it acts like a grader blade and digs in. Over time, we learned to look ahead and, as soon as we saw the track degenerating into a sandy channel, immediately got off onto the harder sand to either side - if there was any there.

The *piste* had descended into a wide dry riverbed, the tracks almost continuously soft and deep. We started to bog down.

Lose speed, have to change into first gear and the front wheel digs into the sand instead of riding on top of it, the rear wheel spins madly, digging you in until you come to a stop. Usually the bike would be so deeply dug in that you could climb off and leave it: it would keep standing on its own. Sometimes we would need to come to each other's assistance, help push to get the bikes going again; sometimes we could get going by pushing the bike and running alongside, feathering the clutch to keep the revs up and then either trying to jump back on or push onto firmer sand when one could start again.

We were quickly becoming exhausted, overheating and consuming our limited supply of water at an alarming rate. At one point we became separated and I shudder to think of what could have happened. The problem is this: once you get unstuck and begin moving, you dare not stop until you reach firmer ground. Controlling the bike and negotiating a way through the soft sand takes all your concentration so it is impossible to be aware of where the other rider is at the same time. At one point both Gareth and I got stuck in deep drifts. Gareth was somewhere ahead of me - I couldn't see him but could hear the revving of his engine. I was exhausted and collapsed next to my bike, deciding I would wait for my big son to walk back and help me. The problem was that Gareth, also bogged down in the sand, thought I was *ahead* of him. He managed to get his bike moving again and pressed on, hoping to overtake me. I was well behind now, waiting. Eventually I recovered sufficiently and decided I would try - one more time - to extricate the bike on my own. I don't know how I got it going again but I did - pushing, feathering the clutch, revving the guts out of the engine to get it moving through the deep sand then leaping on (damn difficult with a load on the back of the bike and two 5-litre cans of fuel strapped behind the foot pegs), battling to get the speed up so the tyres would lift and ride on top of the sand instead of ploughing through... But I made it without dropping the bike again and, a while later, came across Gareth, who had stopped when he heard me behind him. There is no mobile reception that far into the desert, there were tracks going all over the place and we could have lost one another completely. A scary thought.

We wondered what to do. Both of us were exhausted. We had no idea how far this soft sand went - for all we knew it could have been as bad, or even worse, for the next fifty miles. Should we turn back while we still could? And we still had the river to cross. We didn't know how deep it was but we remembered the barely understood warning given us by the local man on his motorbike and the unprecedented flooding we had ridden through when crossing the Atlas. I was concerned I might drop my bike when crossing the river and drown it. It's not a good idea to allow the pistons to suck water into the barrel of an engine. Water cannot compress and the rising piston can crack the barrel - I've seen it happen in Lesotho when one of the riders left his petrol tap on overnight and petrol ran into the barrel; next morning, when he tried to kick-start the engine, the compression split the barrel away from the main engine casing with a crisp *ting!* And that was the end of his engine.

Gareth volunteered to ride ahead and check how far away the crossing of the river - the *Oed* Remila - was. To make it easier, he unloaded his bike and, with a great deal of shoving and an impressive rooster-tail of sand spraying up behind, he set off along the tracks. I collapsed in the shade of a stunted shrub, totally exhausted, and vaguely hoped he would be able to find me again.

A while later, I heard a revving engine and stood to look out for him. As soon as he came into view I could see that he was struggling. The bike was digging in, slewing from side to side between the tracks, and he was having to paddle hard with his legs from time to time to keep it going; at one point the front wheel dug in and he fell but quickly picked the unladen bike up and accelerated hard to reach me. He was so exhausted he could no longer hold the bike up and it fell over.

I have always though of Gareth as a young man with sufficient surplus strength and energy to cope with pretty much anything - but here he was close to his limit. I had never seen him like this before. He lay on his back in the sand, not speaking. I gave him water. After a while he sat up and told me was shattered, his muscles quivering with exhaustion.

Not for the first time, I debated with myself whether we should turn back. I didn't know how much more I could take and our meagre water supplies were diminishing fast. All about us, as far as the eye could see, was this miserable jumble of *chott*, large depressions ridged with what looked like salt crust, skeletal fingers of long-dead trees protruding from the sand, occasional dunes - some the classic Barchan shape, others just random humps or accumulations of sand - and through it all, the soft tracks made their desolate way. We were very hot in our heavy riding gear, constantly thirsty and very tired. But when he had recovered sufficiently to talk, Gareth assured me that the river was only about a mile away and that it looked fordable. The bad news was that between us and the river was soft sand all the way.

We rested a long time, drank more water and discussed our options. We agreed that we'd press on to the river, cross it and see what the desert surface was like on the other side.

Neither of us wanted to turn back.

Then we looked carefully at the track, trying to work out the best way to tackle it without exhausting ourselves or damaging the bikes. Over the past few hours we had started to recognise what the firmer sand looked like and where to find it; we were just beginning to learn to "read" the sand - like a kayaker learns to read the currents in a river and adapts his stroke, body position, angle of approach, to take advantage of it. We had learned quite quickly that to press on in the deep sand of the tracks was going to exhaust us and we would end up overheating the engines or burning out our clutches if we persisted. Off *piste* the land was broken, ridged and chaotic but we were learning how to cross it, to use the curving edge of a dune to get around an obstacle, power over the smaller accumulations in a straight line, the wheels seeming to rise and float over them. (After a while, crossing these became like a game and we were tackling bigger and bigger dunes, keeping our speed up and not allowing the wheels to sink into the sand.)

But in this section of *chott* we realised that the accumulated sand around the base of small, stunted shrubs, raised above the rest of the land, was quite firm. The plan was: firstly, leave the tracks; then, carefully, pick a route from one firm rise to another, using the short downhill run to pick up sufficient speed to get over the soft stuff and up onto the next small, firmer ridge. Pause, scout the land and plan the next rush. After a while, we learned to pick out a route while riding, making our way from firm ridge, across the soft stuff, onto the next section of firm sand, pick up speed, power across a soft section, rest on firm sand, check where the other rider is, move on. We learned to use any rocks, sticks or vegetation to give the wheels extra traction when we started to bog down.

We weren't getting stuck so often any more and in this way, we soon reached the river.

It was wide and stained a muddy brown but seemed fairly shallow. Gareth removed his boots and socks and waded across:

"Firm," he assured me, "but soft in places. I if you wiggle your feet about, they sink."

The sinking bit worried me somewhat.

There were no rocks so we decided to cross at speed, making sure we gave the tyres no time to sink in. To be safe, we decided to unload, carry our kit across and make the crossing unladen. There were three little boys playing in the sand just where we were about to cross; they had been swimming. We'd seen no one for hours, not since the man on the motorbike, not a shack or animal. And yet, here were these three half-naked boys playing in the river. They gathered around us and, when they realised we were about to lug our stuff across, they grabbed as much as they could hold in their skinny little arms and carried it for us. On the other side of the river, after about ten metres of firm, wet sand, the track became very soft again and mounted the river bank, about six or seven foot high. I stood in the water to help if Gareth became stuck and he started his bike, changed quickly into second gear, ramped over the bank and hit the water with a great flurry of spray. He crossed without a problem, accelerated across the firm sand and made it up the soft bank with relative ease.

Then it was my turn. I too unpacked, the little boys enthusiastically carried my kit across and, with Gareth standing on the opposite bank, I selected first gear and accelerated. To my consternation, the back wheel just dug in and I struggled to pick up speed and get the bike into second. But at last the rear wheel rose to the surface, I picked up speed and made it across without incident, hitting the soft sand of the far bank and skidding to the top. We gave the little boys some money for their help, reloaded and set off again.

It was getting late now, we were very tired and we decided to look for a place to camp. But we still had to cross a belt of soft sand a few miles wide, this time interspersed with low dunes. We picked our way through, gaining experience all the time on how to cope with the sand, learning how to read the desert surface, recognise the very soft parts and avoid them if possible and, if not, how to power across them without sinking in or falling over.

Finally, ahead of me, I saw the ground change: the colour turned black and I knew we had almost reached a gravel plain locally known as *reg*, a section of flat desert covered with a layer of round black pebbles no bigger than your fist, firm sand beneath and great for riding over. I picked my way through the last of the soft sand, around the last dunes and felt the smooth, firm surface beneath my wheels.

I had made it. I stopped and waited for Gareth.

The sun was low on the horizon; every muscle ached, but soon we would be setting up camp, preparing a meal, drinking tea and reflecting on the day in the comfort of our tents.

But Gareth was still battling through the sand. I sat on my bike, watching him. He only had about thirty metres to go and I was sure he would be alongside me in seconds.

One more dune to cross...

As I watched, he accelerated up the face of the dune and the bike stopped as if he had hit a brick wall. He almost went over the handlebars. I waited for him to extricate himself but he didn't move. In the end I got off my bike and walked to where he was stuck. His bike was deeply sunk into the sand, up to the engine, and there was no way it was going to move forward up the slope of the dune face. We tried to pull it back but it was as if fixed in concrete. And yet, it was a perfectly normal looking dune face. And so we learned, as many desert travellers have learned before us, that there are deceptive soft patches in the sand which act almost like water into which a foot or vehicle just sinks. The two of us, working together, could not budge the heavy KTM an inch. In the end we had to lie it on its side and drag it around before Gareth could pick it up again and ride it onto the firm ground via a different route.

The day was almost over. A cool wind had sprung up, lifting the sand and blowing it in little stinging cascades across the ground and over the steep leeward slopes of dunes. Shadows lengthened across the desolate landscape all around us.

We rode on, the ground becoming increasingly rocky; by now we had lost the main track but knew we were approximately where we should be so were not worried. We would find the track again the next day. On the lower slope of a smooth-sided *massif*, capped with the distinctive black rock found in the area, we saw a lone acacia tree and made for it. There was soft sand nearby so we decided to stop for the night. We unpacked, stripped off our shirts and revelled in the cool evening air. Soon our tents were up and water boiling for tea. And as the sun began to set, the two of us climbed to the top of the mountain that overshadowed our camp and sat in quiet contemplation, watching colour leach from the land, the sky turning deep orange and then red before darkness set in.

And, sitting on a rock high above the desert plain watching the last of the light leach from the sky, I was filled with a deep sense of peace. We hadn't turned back. We had made it through. We had learned.

Tomorrow would be easier.

With the sun now below the horizon, the land took on a softness and the air cooled. I looked out at the vastness of the desert far below stretching in pale but darkening shades of brown and cream and grey and black and red - and I thanked God for looking after us, for my son at my side, for the privilege of what I was experiencing.

Reluctantly we made our way down the mountain in the semi-darkness, slipping as the loose scree broke away, the rocks clinking together with a strange metallic note. Back at the tents we prepared supper of instant soup and the salami that the cats hadn't eaten. We sipped at cups of coffee, feeling the pain ooze out of our muscles.

Later the wind died and the desert was totally silent, the sky bright with stars.

It had taken us five hours to cover forty-five miles.

Day two in the desert

Early the next morning, before the sun rose, we got up, made tea and then climbed to the top of the rocky *massif* in whose shadow we had spent the night. High above the desert surface we sat quietly watching the sun rise. It was fairly overcast so the effect was not as dramatic as the blood-soaked sunset the night before, but the vast desolation of the desert was almost palpable as detail slowly emerged from the darkness, rocks and dunes and the dark range of mountains that had followed us for so long slowly taking form; far below us the landscape shifted and changed as the light gave it substance.

A special moment.

But we were looking forward with anticipation to the day so made our way down, packed up the tents, loaded the bikes and set off again, hoping to make the most of the early morning coolness.

It took a while to find a clear *piste,* but I was happy to rely on Gareth's navigation skills as we made our way across reasonably firm sand in the general direction we should be heading. We were following the bed of an ancient watercourse - the Kerb Azougg-Ouarh - in places at lcast two miles wide (although it's so difficult to estimate distances in the emptiness of the desert) that threaded its way between the dark-topped mountains on either side of us. Sometimes a lone *massif* would rise out of the wide, flat plain, almost perfectly conical in shape, but usually they ran in long parallel ridges, flat-topped and rocky, devoid of vegetation.

Other than the thick groves of palms in the oases or along some river beds where the water is close to the surface, the only vegetation we came across in this section of desert were occasional gnarled tamarisk and acacia trees, thorny and twisted, which follow underground river beds where their deep roots can reach the water. How they manage to survive in this forbidding landscape I cannot imagine. But one is so often surprised by delicate touches of life in amongst the harsh sterility of sand and rock, like flowers blooming from between the cracks in a rock, insects and birds carrying on with their busy little lives despite the harshness and apparent sterility of the desert around them.

We hoped to find firm going after the struggle we had had the day before, but after an initial kilometre of firm sand (just to lull us into a false sense of security, I suppose) we hit the soft stuff again and battled our way for the next hour looking for the right track. But this time we didn't get stuck. Not once. The previous day's ride had been a baptism of fire; we had learned our lessons well and continued to make steady progress.

We finally left the soft sand behind and the track led us onto the bed of a dry lake. What bliss after the past day and a half of struggle. For twenty miles Gareth and I sped together across a smooth surface at over sixty miles an hour. We could have gone faster but wisdom prevailed. It was a joyous time and we revelled in the freedom it gave, looping this way and that across the smooth surface, feeling the rush of cool air against our faces. Sadly, the lake bed came to an end and the track led us over a rocky landscape with many nasty dips where, during floods, small streams had cut deep channels across the track. At first I took these too fast and my bike bottomed out a number of times. Fortunately my bash plate took most of the beating but when I removed it later that evening it had been knocked about quite badly and I had to bash it back into shape with a rock. One of the impacts had bent my side stand mounting a little and others had knocked off a few of the aluminium cooling fins under the engine but other than that, no significant damage, fortunately. I realised how easy it would be for a rock to smash through the thin aluminium of my sump and leave us stranded.

To talk bikes for a moment, I have nothing but admiration for my KLE500. By the end of this trip - five thousand three hundred miles - it had taken quite a battering but sustained no significant damage other than a broken choke cable. For next time, and for any of you who are thinking of doing a ride like this, do yourself a favour and make sure your bike has a robust bash plate protecting the underside of the whole engine. The bash plate fitted as standard to the KLE is a Mickey-Mouse thing, about 1mm thick aluminium that I can bend with my fingers. I will replace it with a robust plate of at least 3mm extending back to protect the rear of the engine, which the standard plate doesn't. It did the job, but was pretty battered by the end of the trip. The KLE's ride height is just a little too low for serious rocky terrain when carrying a heavy load and it bottomed out many times. You might consider upgrading the suspension as well. Gareth's KTM990 loved the rocky stuff; its higher ground clearance meant that his retro-fitted Black Dog bash plate only took a few knocks. But that added height makes the bike just too high for me. You really don't want to try to ride a laden bike through large rocks or soft sand if you can't put your feet flat on the ground at rest. If when seated only your toes touch the ground you *will* fall over. The slightest unevenness in the terrain - rocks, sand, small *oeds* crossing the road - will have you over if you lose balance and can't ride out of trouble. A bike that size with heavy load is simply impossible to hold up with one leg if it decides it wants to lie down. Gareth is 6'4 and very strong but many times on this trip he simply didn't have the strength to hold the KTM up. So, I'll trade a lower clearance with a greater ability to keep the bike's wheels where they ought to be, thank you. In the soft sand, the Kawasaki was far easier to ride; it just didn't dig in as quickly as the KTM; but in the rocks, the KTM was king.

Finally, after an exhilarating hundred miles we finally reached the outskirts of Zagora. Just after Gareth had hit a soft ridge in the road and come off - again! - we were flagged down by two Moroccan men in a Land Rover - the first people we had seen for the whole day.

They were from a garage in Zagora and, I think, were out roaming, looking for business. In a fashion so typical of this country, they insisted we come to their garage and have a cup of tea (they promptly pasted stickers advertising their garage on our windscreens - and throughout the rest of the trip, anyone we met who had passed thorough Zagora had a similar sticker pasted on their bike or 4X4.) They led us up some back streets through the town, parked us outside their garage - a most impressive set-up - and sent off for tea. (It was called the Garage Iriki Mazuga - if you ever have car or bike trouble around Mazuga, these are the guys to contact. A great bunch.)

Gareth and I stripped our jackets off and splashed ice-cold water over our heads and faces from a tap in the workshop. My side stand wouldn't fully extend causing my bike to want to fall over whenever we stopped so I asked them to look at it. They got out a rotary cutting blade and trimmed a small piece of metal away, allowing the stand to fully deploy. When I asked what I owed them for the work, they smiled and waved me away. In the end, I gave them a tenner, we had tea and left to find a campsite.

We set up our tents at a pleasant, shady site where we met a bunch of Belgians and a Frenchman who had travelled extensively around Morocco. The Frenchman, Luc, had ridden the *piste* we had just completed a few years before on an old XT500. He told us that on the way he ran out of oil and the engine seized. He was travelling with a 4X4 support vehicle carrying his luggage and spares so they waited for the engine to cool, filled the sump with oil, started her up and completed the *piste*. What amazing bikes, those old XT500s. Unkillable.

Later that evening we met the Belgians in town and they led us around the back of a hotel to a small bar where we sank an over priced beer or two. Although a Moslem country and supposedly alcohol free, small pubs like this one are hidden away in back streets and the authorities seem to turn a blind eye. It made me feel as if we were creeping off for a quick smoke behind the bike sheds at school.

While discussing our route, our Belgian friend warned us against attempting the *piste* we planned to tackle the next day. He insisted it was very soft for most of the way and we wouldn't make it. Throughout this section of desert, he warned, we would come across treacherous red-coloured sand, so bad they had battled to get through in a 4X4.

This was worrying. The *piste* we planned to follow the next day was nearly twice the distance of the one we had just covered and if we were to encounter even worse sand for most of the way, we were in for some serious trouble.

Later, on our own, Gareth and I discussed our options. There was another, shorter track, marked as a better road on the map that we could take. But in the end we decided to give it a go. If we found it too difficult, we could always turn back.

A brief diversion - Riding in sand

I'm going to diverge a little here and write about riding a laden bike in soft sand. If you are not interested or you did the Dakar last year - please feel free to skip ahead.

There are bikers out there who make riding in soft sand look easy. We've all seen the Dakar riders chewing up the soft stuff and sending rooster-tails into the faces of their competitors, flying along across a flat desert at a hundred miles an hour. (Well, I assume you've seen them.) But we've also seen them in despair lying exhausted in the sand with a deeply dug-in bike. We've watched them waving nonchalantly at the TV helicopter before flying fifty metres through the air and breaking all their bones when they hit a cunningly hidden dry river bed that the route planners failed to tell them about because cart wheeling bikes and competitors flying through the air makes for good TV.

So, this section is for ordinary blokes like you and me who might think of doing a bit of desert riding in the future.

The trick is quite simple - *speed*.

If you've got the balls, the faster you ride, the easier any vehicle travels over soft sand. I've seen bikers riding their bikes over *water* (without prior prayer) - you've just got to go fast enough to get the bike aquaplaning. Look on You Tube - it's worth a watch.

Of course, the faster you ride the further you will fly through the air when you hit something (and you probably will) so use your discretion here.

And for speed, you need to select a higher gear. Trying to battle your way through soft sand in first gear will get you nowhere; your engine will overheat and seize and you will be exhausted before you have covered a mile. Use first gear only to get the bike moving; use your legs and paddle the bike along if the back wheel starts digging in. Keep the revs as high as you feel is safe and then kick it into second. You must do this quickly. Your revs mustn't drop. You will probably wince at what it's doing to your engine, clutch and gearbox but most modern bikes can cope with a bit of flogging from time to time, so just hit it. If you pause, even ever so briefly when changing up, your bike will stop, wheels deep in the sand, and when you release the clutch your engine will die.

If you have selected second gear and your revs begin to drop, I found feathering my clutch briefly to keep up the revs worked well - but only briefly or you could burn out your clutch. As soon as you begin to pick up speed in second, you should feel the bike begin to rise on top of the sand and you're on your way. Select third if you can.

Be careful. Don't be overcome with a sense of *joie de vivre* and open her up over an unknown *piste* - I did and it could have killed me. But that was later.

Crossing dunes can be great fun once you get the knack. The key is selecting the right speed and knowing when to cut the revs. If you go too fast you will fly over the crest and break all your bones. If you bottle it and slow down too early, your bike will dig in before you are over the crest. And, trust me, a dug-in bike half way up a dune is *very* difficult to get out. You cannot go forward. It's too steep and too soft. If you've dug your back wheel in deep you can't push it out backwards either. A bunch of strong mates all pushing and pulling together might get it moving. If you're on your own, or even with two of you, as Gareth and I found on a few occasions, you will probably not budge it. Lie the bike on its side, drag it round by pulling on the front wheel and, once it is facing downhill, pick it up again. It can usually be ridden out then.

If you hit the dune just right, it's like a fairground ride. At the correct speed, your wheels seem to float lightly over the sand - and you immediately look for more dunes so you can do it again. This is *such* fun! But, be warned: Barchan dunes have a windward slope of about 15° and a slip face of 32° (I checked it in Wickapedia); get it wrong and you could find yourself riding at speed at a 32° slope and you'll hit it like brick wall; misread a Barchan dune for a small whale-back of sand and you'll find yourself flying off a 32° sand cliff (as I did). It's very hard to judge angles when you're looking at accumulations of sand piled on top of vast acres of sand the same colour. Your eyes have difficulty working out perspective, just like when you're walking across a field of virgin snow.

Try not to stop. Look ahead and select the correct gear (usually second or third) *before* you reach the soft stuff, accelerate hard and keep the revs up until you reach firm ground then change up and give the engine a breather.

If you do stop in deep sand you are in trouble. You've got a number of options, all of which we used and found to work:

1. Take a strong son along with you and wait until he notices you are no longer behind him, stops, walks back and gives you a push. One person pushing is usually enough to get a bike going again.

2. No big son to push you: Engage first gear, get legs ready to paddle like mad, rev the engine *hard*; drop the clutch. You will know within seconds whether this is working. If you don't start moving at a pace you know will enable you to select second gear, *do not* keep on spinning the back wheel. All experienced 4X4 drivers know this. Keep spinning the wheels and all you're doing is giving yourself a great deal of extra work digging the bike out of where it's buried itself in the sand. A spinning wheel not moving forwards in soft sand is digging itself *down*. And you don't want to end up with your engine nestled in the sand. So, if you're not moving forward paddling with your legs and spinning the back wheel, then

3. Get off the bike and wait for the son to walk back. Or, get off the bike, select first gear, rev her up, drop the clutch and push, running alongside. You either keep this up until you reach firm ground (very exhausting) or try to leap on while you are moving. This is particularly difficult if you've got a load on the rear of the bike, which you will have if you're travelling. It's always good to keep a finger or two on the clutch so you can feather it briefly to keep up the revs or, more probably, to disengage the clutch when you trip in the sand and the bike falls on top of you.

4. You could let down your tyres. This gives a wider footprint and, like a camel's foot, spreads the load over a greater area of sand and the wheel doesn't dig in as far. I suggested this to Gareth when we were battling on the first day but he counselled against it because our tyres did not have rim locks; let the tyres down too far and you could spin the rim inside the tyre which will rip the valve out of the tube and, if you don't have a spare, you're stuffed because you can't patch that.

5. Last option, unload the bike and dig away the sand in front of both wheels. This will usually do the trick. The down side is that you then have to walk back and carry

your stuff to the bike and reload, cursing yourself all the while for bringing too much luggage.

If none of the above works, you're buggered, mate. Leave the bike and walk out. Go look for help. Promise yourself you'll never go riding in deep sand again on your own, without at least one strong mate who can help you when things get bad.

So, that's my layman's advice on riding a heavily laden bike in deep sand, written from all the experience of a four-week trip into Morocco. Hope it doesn't sound too condescending. Most of you probably know all this anyway.

A good friend of mine in South Africa gave me this advice, rather more succinct than mine and just as valid: *Look up, stand up and open up.*

But I did give you the option of skipping on, didn't I?

The desert...

The next day's ride across the desert from Mhamid to Foum-Zguid was, without doubt, our most memorable. Merely attempting to put it into words leaves me feeling inadequate. Whatever I write will fall far short of the evanescent images I carry with me in my head.

In a way, translating our day-long adventure from the reality it was into sterile, dry words is like when you are travelling in some exotic location and you stumble across a panoramic vista so beautiful that for a moment you forget to breathe, and you think: *I have* got *to capture this. This is* so *beautiful,* so *amazing - I* must *show people back home!* But when you put the camera to your eye, a sadness, a disappointment comes over you because you realise that the view in front of you, which fills your whole world, is just too wide, too multi-faceted, too nuanced for a mere snapshot to do it justice. And in the end you put the camera away, just stand in awe and look and absorb, hoping that enough of the image will imprint on your brain for later recall when the mundane greyness of life presses down upon you.

That's how I feel.

The images I carry with me took one hundred and forty miles and seven hours to form. Throughout the day, as I was riding, I asked myself: How can I recapture this in a way that will bring it alive in the minds of those who haven't been here?

As soon as we stopped for the night, I took out pen and paper, quickly jotting down disparate, fleeting images, without any attempt at chronology, trying to hold them before they disappeared...

Nuances of shade and colour in the sand and rock; desert textures - fine, rough, ordered, chaotic, ridged with salt-crust; a broken and wind-swept landscape blends seamlessly into hidden valleys gentled with acacia trees; the smoothness of an ancient lake-bed followed by long struggles with soft sand; rolling hills tessellated with smooth black stones, so ordered it could be a mosaic; salt pans, still wet and yielding under our tyres, the surface cracked and wrinkled like elephant-skin; fine, milky, wind-blown dust so thick that the lower half of a body or motorbike simply disappears below waist height and strange half-people move mysteriously, seemingly unconnected with the ground; crisp-edged dunes lie on the hard desert surface, sculpted by the wind's hand; gnarled acacia trees, lonely patriarchs, seem to crouch and writhe against the heat, standing incongruous in the sand - disparate images flicker through my mind, blend and come together, separate and coalesce like slides flashed briefly against a wall and then they blend again...

Of course, I could just write, "Today Gareth and I rode for seven hours over one hundred and forty miles of desert," and leave it at that.

Part of me wants to because the memories are so vivid, so special, that trying to capture them, alive and breathing, and pin them onto a page with words seems to take something from them, suck the life out of them, turn the three dimensions into two. And when you thrust a pin with rough hands through the abdomen of a butterfly, crush out its life and set up for display, ask the world to look at it and wonder, its iridescence becomes dull and lifeless; somehow it loses something, an intangible nothingness that is, in fact, its essence.

I'd like to say that the desert was "trackless", use that adjective to conjure up images of endless, graceful dunes disappearing to the horizon under a burning sun; lonely travellers lost in a world of undulating sand.

But it wasn't like that.

It was more *real*.

There *were* tracks.

And then sometimes there weren't and it seemed like we were the last people in an empty world with only the wind and the scutter of blown sand grains to keep us company.

Often the tracks were just tyre marks in the sand that branched and came together in a seemingly random manner. Sometimes they coalesced into something resembling a "road", then the tyre marks would slowly disappear; or they might meet a sand dune that had not been there when they were first made, had grown and migrated in its inexorable way, blocking the path so, over time, successive drivers would need to deviate again and again to find a way round.

Many times that day we rode for miles across literally trackless sections of desert *reg*, which varied in colour and surface texture again and yet again throughout the day, its changing mood affecting our mood as we rode, subtle differences that we would notice not only by sight but also by feel as our tyres skimmed across miles of silky-smooth, dry lake-bed, bit and slewed through deep soft sand, moved with a disconcerting sway from side to side across vast salt flats of slightly damp, muddy plain where one was never quite sure when the bikes might suddenly sink under, dig in and throw you over the handle bars; we picked our way through rolling ridges covered with sharp rocks that would rip a tyre if hit too hard but then these ridges would suddenly become smooth and gentle, covered in almost mathematical precision with tiny finger-nail sized stones, black as jet, the sand beneath slightly soft and yielding so one could ride across these swelling ocean waves of sand at speed and feel quite safe; then there were horrible sections, tens of miles wide, where the ground seemed to have been stirred up whilst still wet, leaving sharp ridges of dried mud interspersed with strange round hollows three metres across, the whole area spiked with the skeletal remains of long-dead bushes bleached white by the sun. We would have to pick our way over these at no more than walking pace to prevent damage to the bikes. It was in this churned-up ground where we usually found the dunes - not the massive ones you see on postcards, but a jumbled mix of perfectly shaped Barchans, no more than ten foot high but usually lower, others formed into long random ridges with channels of firm sand between. We came across soft dunes, humped and red, on a white-grey desert floor, whale-backs of sand protruding through an ocean of more sand, the curves so gentle that you could ride across them with a quick burst of speed, feel the tyres hesitate briefly then rise to the surface and skim, smooth as a fish, until you dipped back onto the rough harder surface on the other side.

The difficult times were when the dunes completely blocked the way for as far as one could see. Usually you can pick your way around and through dune belts, keeping on mostly firm sand, but sometimes this is not possible and you have no choice but to force your way over them. Some of these sand ridges were relatively short - twenty metres or so - and could be crossed with a good burst of speed; but the difficult crossings were where the thick sand stretched for fifty metres or more, where the route through was not straight but curved, making its way around and in between the clutter of dunes so you couldn't get a good run at it. This became especially difficult when a group of

4X4s had churned up the ground and, just in front of you, one was driving ponderously through the thick sand, blocking your path so you knew that if you didn't blast your way around you would slow and dig in.

But the group of 4X4s we met that day is another story.

Let me start at the beginning ...

Our nefarious desert guide

We got away from our campsite in Zagora early, thinking of Luc's warning that we would be unwise to tackle the *piste* from Mhamid to Foum-Zguid because of very bad soft sand. I must admit, after our struggle over the last two days getting the laden bikes through the sand from Merzouga, I was apprehensive. But we agreed that we'd give it a try and, if it became too bad, we'd turn back.

The road to Mhamid was good, just a narrow strip of tar crumbling at the edges, wide enough, really, for just one car. Reaching the town, we filled up our tanks plus spare fuel containers, topped up our four litres of water each and headed out of town, looking for the track. But it wasn't long before a 4X4, driven by a local man, flagged us down. He asked us where we were going.

We told him: "Foum-Zguid."

"It is impossible," he warned, leaning out of the window of his truck. "You cannot go. The *piste* is flooded."

We looked at him, incredulous. This was the desert. It's supposed to be dry. We were suspicious and reluctant to believe him.

Seeing our doubt, he added, "Already this morning there have been two trucks stuck in the mud. We have rescued them."

Ironic, really, that it wasn't the sand that was going to stop us, it was water.

But, in Africa, there is always a way around impediments - especially if money is involved. He told us that he knew a local Tuareg guide who could lead us around the flooded section of the Draa River valley, taking us into the dunes above the riverbed over higher ground. For two hundred Euro he would carry all our luggage in his truck and lead us forty miles around the flooded section and leave us on a clear *piste,* marked with cairns, that was once part of the Pari-Dakar rally route. "You can follow them to Foum-Zguid - easy..."

Gareth and I were torn. We so badly wanted to do this; in fact, I think we both knew that we *were* going to do it - what an adventure! - but we felt the price was way too high and, more important, we just didn't trust this guy. He had a smoothness about him, an easy patter that just shouted: *Lying, cheating bas**rd* . We even doubted his story about the flooded riverbed; had he made it up just to dupe us out of our money?

We debated whether we should just find the track, follow it until we reached the water and then see. If it were impassable, like he said, we would turn back and take him up on his offer.

But it was getting late. If we did this, there would probably not be enough time to complete the ride to Foum-Zguid that day and we would have to wait until the next to attempt it.

The driver, waiting for a decision, added with undeniable logic, "Is cheaper you pay me two hundred now. More expensive if later I rescue you when you stuck."

He was right. If we did need to call someone out to extricate bikes and luggage mired in mud deep in the desert, there is no knowing what they would charge. They'd have us over a barrel.

We still didn't trust him but felt we couldn't pass up this opportunity. Being led through the open desert by a Tuareg guide, having our luggage carried in a 4X4 that would free us up to enjoy the riding was too good an opportunity to pass up.

So we haggled. In the end, we settled on a price of one hundred and twenty-five Euros. We reiterated the conditions, just so there would be no misunderstanding later: "You will lead us into the dunes around the flooded section?"

"Yes."

"For forty miles?"

"Yes."

"And you will leave us on a track that will take us to Form-Zguid - a track with cairns? A Pari-Dakar track?"

"Yes."

We were still suspicious, so we tried to get him to accept half the money before we left and the rest when he had delivered his part of the bargain - but he categorically refused.

In the end, our desire to attempt this trek through the dunes overcame our natural caution and we agreed. We followed him down a small back alley where the money changed hands. Gareth thought this was suspicious in itself - why not in the open, in an office? Why down a back street with money passed almost surreptitiously through a low wooden door to some faceless individual half hidden in darkness?

While we waited for our guide, I bought some oranges at a roadside stall - which turned out to be a life-saver during the rest of the day, a wonderful burst of liquid and flavour that clears the head and quenches thirst. We packed our luggage into the back of the 4X4; our pale-skinned guide arrived and climbed into the passenger seat. Like most Tuareg Berbers he was thin and wiry, his head almost completely wrapped in a blue *tagelmust,* which he would unwrap to protect his face from blown sand, long, yellow teeth and a thin, aquiline nose.

All our luggage stowed away in the back of the 4X4, and with a sense of excitement tightening the chest, we left the outskirts of Mhamid, which soon disappeared into the haze of sand being blown off the desert surface by a strong wind, and made our way across a flat, barren landscape of *reg*, wind-blown and stony. But it wasn't long before we encountered the dunes, at first small and isolated so we could make our way around them, keeping to the firmer ground. I wanted to slow down, enjoy the experience, stop and take photographs, but our driver seemed to be in a hurry, disappearing ahead of us into the milky, wind-blown sand, dodging around small dunes at a fast pace. It seemed he wanted to get our forty miles done as quickly as possible and then rush back to rip off some other gullible bikers. We had to ride hard to keep up with him.

Soon the dunes increased and our guide was having difficulty finding the way. At times the 4X4 seemed to be driving about aimlessly, looking for a way through. We followed as best we could. Then I saw the 4X4 pause then head straight at a steep-faced dune and grind his way over before heading off into the sand-haze. There was no way around.

I was worried I would get stuck and be left behind. With the truck rapidly disappearing, I approached the dune, keeping out of its deep tracks, and accelerated up the face. Then I made the classic error of all desert novices: I misjudged my speed, lost my nerve half way up, tapped off a fraction too early and immediately dug in just below the crest, the engine nestled deeply into the soft sand of the ridge.

Bugger!

Ahead and below me, the truck and Gareth continued on, into the smudged, wind-blown barrenness that stretched across the horizon in front of me, unaware of the fact that I was badly stuck and immobile. Frightened now, I managed - with a great deal of gut-wrenching - to drag the unladen bike out of the sand down the dune face and tried again, giving myself a good run up this time and keeping the power on until I had crested the dune ridge before tapping off to slide gently down the windward face. I was shaking, still apprehensive as I tried to keep Gareth and the 4X4 in sight as they disappeared behind even more dunes; the wind was blowing hard now and visibility was severely reduced.

As I raced to catch up, a number of questions fluttered about in my brain: If I'd stuck on my *first* dune, what was it going to be like later? Would I be able to cope? What if they had driven on, deep into the wilderness of sand, and couldn't find me when they finally realised I wasn't there and turned back? Would we be able to follow the *piste* he was going to leave us on without getting lost? Were we being wise, especially as we didn't particularly trust this guy who now had all our luggage and money?

(Later during our trip we met other bikers who had stories to tell about predatory "guides" who would lead bikers into deep sand and, when they were hopelessly stuck, demand more money to get them out. Whether these are just travellers' tales I don't know, but I wouldn't put it past some of the more unscrupulous desert entrepreneurs. Other than our slimy bas**rd and a few corrupt policemen, we had nothing but good treatment from the generous and hospitable Moroccan people we met.)

But I soon got the hang of it and started to enjoy myself. Gareth and I were revelling in the freedom of riding through often trackless desert, over and around dunes, on responsive bikes freed from the impediment of our luggage. Often we would branch aside from the tracks of the 4X4 and make our own way, keeping it in sight, picking our way through the dunes, learning to read the sand and the surface, gaining confidence.

At one point, pausing to take a photograph, Gareth drew my attention to something almost lost in the driven sand behind us: a column of orange vehicles was meandering its way through the dunes. And for the next hour, each time we paused and looked back, they were there. Obviously their guide and our guide were leading us in approximately the same direction.

Then our 4X4 driver stopped, switched off the engine and seemed to be waiting. He didn't communicate with us. The guide, face partly hidden by his blue *tagelmust,* sat in the vehicle, immersed in his own thoughts. The group of orange 4X4s slowly approached and stopped next to us. Animated conversation between our driver and theirs. Finally our driver walked over and informed us that the driver and guide of the seven Land Cruisers were friends of his and they would lead us from here on.

Gareth checked on his GPS - this slimy git had led us a mere thirteen miles before dumping us on one of his so-called friends. I was furious and demanded he fulfil his obligation. I asked for part of our money back. He refused. I told him he was cheating us and that it was for this very reason we had wanted to keep half the money back and pay him when he had done what he contracted with us to do.

He tried to assure us that it was all fine. We were unimpressed and continued to tell him what we thought of him, trying to get him to give us some of our money back.

But there was little we could do. Our money had already been handed over to a man inside a dark hut somewhere in a back alley. We'd been had.

The other driver and guide assured us that it was OK, they would take us. It was, in the universally known phrase, "No problem."

But there *was* a problem. We had no contract, verbal or otherwise, with these two total strangers who were about to take responsibility for leading us across another one hundred and thirty-odd miles of desert. Furthermore, they had been hired by the Land Cruiser drivers, not us. Who were we to muscle in on their trip? What would happen if we broke down?

I went up to a group of men - all Belgians - and told them our problem and asked whether they would be prepared for us to tag along with them. They said it was not a problem. This was good of them because, as is universally accepted in any extreme environment, the moment someone joins your group you automatically assume responsibility for them. In the same way that, if any of the Toyotas had broken down we would assist them in any way we could, by agreeing to us joining them, they were equally taking responsibility to look after us if either of us broke down. It's unlikely they would have needed any help from us because the Land Cruisers were almost new, all identical and supported by a Unimog with all the tools and spares they would ever need. But they all seemed quite happy to have us and, feeling both embarrassed and relieved, we transferred our luggage into their guide's 4X4.

In a way, our dishonest driver did us a favour. He had contracted to lead us forty miles and then, supposedly, abandon us on track marked with cairns that would lead us, eventually (hopefully), to Foum-Zguid. Well, we rode with the Toyotas for the rest of the day and into the evening, covering one hundred and forty miles and there was no clear track *anywhere*. It is unlikely that we would have found our way through on our own. At what point we would have turned round and whether we would have had sufficient fuel to get back, I don't know.

But we were lucky.

Finally, luggage packed in the Ford 4X4, permission to join the Land Cruisers granted, we set off again, very conscious that we were guests, in a way, and would need to maintain pace with them and not hold them up. As it turned out, this was not a problem because the drivers of the seven short-wheel base Land Cruisers had obviously been given strict instructions to keep in line and, as was clear later in the day when one of them got stuck when trying to cross a fairly small dune, they had little experience of driving in sand. So their progress was somewhat plodding throughout the day, driving nose to tail, often shrouded in each other's dust. They stopped only four times - usually when their guide lost his way and left us while he drove around through the dunes, looking for a way out. This gave Gareth and me the freedom to range about on either side of them, racing ahead when the going was good, playing and having fun in the varied conditions we encountered throughout the day.

A little about our Belgian friends:

A shipload of brand new short wheel base Land Cruisers caught fire en route during delivery and there was some damage to the cabs of a number of the vehicles. A group of Belgian men decided to buy seven of these fire-damaged 4X4s - I would imagine for a song - from the insurance company; they then set up a company, *Africa Overland,* spent a great deal of money rebuilding the interior of the cars including custom-made dashboards, fitted mini fridges, bull bars, resprayed all the Cruisers a deep burnt orange, all the bells and whistles; they purchased a brand new Unimog as a backup vehicle and equipped it with tools, spares, air compressor - all you would need for desert travel. When we came across them, they were taking the Cruisers on a test run across the desert to make sure everything was ship-shape before they started commercial operations. We got to know some of them quite well by the end of the day (we stayed in the same hotel as they did that night and spoke to them at length in the bar where they made serious inroads into the alcohol stocks).

Actually, instead of being a burden on them - fortunately neither Gareth nor I got sufficiently badly stuck throughout the day to cause them delay nor did we have any breakdowns - a number of them said how much they had enjoyed having us with them. In fact, they told us how frustrated they felt being forced to drive slowly, in a straight line one behind the other, while we raced about the desert all around them, obviously enjoying ourselves. A few of them were bikers too and they just wanted to get out of the 4X4s and onto a bike!

One comment was made that sticks in my mind because, in a way, it has a special metaphorical resonance for me: That evening in the hotel bar, whiskey in hand, one of the Belgian drivers told us that the most memorable part of the day for him was seeing Gareth and me riding alongside each other along a wide, flat stretch of desert, "drifting in unison". I have no memory of *drifting* together with Gareth; certainly it was not done intentionally. And when riding at speed on a loose surface, the rear wheel will naturally drift depending on how sharply one turns and how much one spins the rear wheel. But immediately he said that, I thought to myself: What an apt metaphor - Gareth and me, father and son, *drifting* together in unison across the desert...

I had two close calls on that day's riding that could have ended in tragedy. After both near accidents I was very aware just how lucky I had been; if something had happened just a little differently I could have had a serious accident, broken bones, my neck, or seriously damaged the bike. After close calls like these, in times of sober reflection afterwards, I find it prompts me to think about the tenuousness of life and how we should live in the short time we are allotted...

Anyway, this is how they nearly happened:

As I have mentioned before, the only way to get through really soft sand is to take it at speed. During the day we had to make our way through a number of dune belts, some of them kilometres wide. Often, we could find a way through and between the individual dunes without having to cross any but sometimes the sand lay unbroken right across our path and there was no alternative but to battle our way through it. But the problem was that we were riding with these seven Land Cruisers and the Unimog, driving nose to tail, and we *had* to stay in front of the last vehicle in case we got stuck or broke down and they inadvertently left us behind. So, when it came to crossing a section of sand we would take our place in the line of 4X4s, slow or stop the vehicles behind us to allow a gap to open up and then accelerate through the sand, building up sufficient speed to get across. Unfortunately, during one crossing the sand was much longer than I had anticipated and the deep tracks cut by the Cruisers in front made several turns around the bases of dunes before reaching firm ground again. Because I wasn't able to see around the first dune, I was not aware that the stretch of soft sand was much longer than any we had crossed before. I duly took my place in the line of 4X4s; stopped to allow a gap to form; when I thought there was enough distance between me and the truck in front to enable me to get through at a decent speed, I accelerated, changed into second and went for it. The sand was very soft and had been churned up by the Land Cruisers that had already made it through. As I rounded the first dune, however, I suddenly became aware that the deep sand continued around at least another dune and I was fast closing the gap between me and the Land Cruiser in front. I had to make a quick decision: either I slowed down behind him, when I would sink into his tracks and block the following Cruisers or I would have to overtake. I glanced up and saw that the dune in front had a concave slope just perfect to take me around the Land Cruiser and enable me to get ahead of him. I kept my throttle wide open, left the deep tracks, used the concave slope like a high berm and shot past the 4X4 - only to realise too late that right in front of me the dune dropped off like a small cliff.

There was nothing I could do. I ramped over the drop - I suppose it was about 4 ft high - thinking as I flew through the air: *This is it! You're a gonner* - landed on my front wheel and, for some reason, didn't go head over heels. (I've been head over heels before on a bike, during an enduro many years before - the bike landed full on my chest and did unpleasant things to my ribs and sternum and I always dread it happening again.) I know the rear-view mirror hit me hard in the chest; I just managed to get back control of the bike with a little flailing of legs, hit the deep ruts now turning sharp left around the other side of the dune and promptly dropped the bike. Slowly and ponderously, the Land Cruiser I had just overtaken ploughed its way past me through the soft sand as I struggled to pick up my bike, feeling like a prat.

That evening, in the bar, the driver told me that, when he saw me fly over the edge of the dune, he quipped to his co-driver, "Shall we run over him, drive round him or call an ambulance?"

Later that afternoon my luck held again. We had come to some vast dry lake beds, locally called *chotts* (well, some were hard, dry and smooth; others were wet and slightly rough, but we could ride over both surfaces at speed). These stretched for miles in every direction and Gareth and I were in our element. We would lag back to allow the 4X4s to get well ahead then speed past, standing on the pegs, taking great loops to either side of them as they made their ponderous way, like wingless flying ants, one behind the other. The dry surface was devoid of any obstructions - no stones, twigs, ripples, nothing at all other than perfectly smooth sand. And we were seduced. It was such fun! We were riding across expanses of the Sahara with no tracks, no tyre marks, just this dead flat surface in every direction stretching almost to the horizon.

And it was while riding at seventy miles an hour that I hit the dune.

Granted, it was a small one, just a whale-back of sand on an otherwise featureless plain, the same colour as the rest of the ground so it was impossible to see from any distance away. I suppose I saw it just before I hit it, I can't really remember. What I do remember is hitting the dune, hard, so my suspension bottomed out, and then I was in the air. And while I was in the air I can remember wondering how badly I was going to be injured when I hit the ground and high-sided. I seemed to be in the air for ages but I suppose it wasn't. Everything seemed to slow down. Then I hit, again bottomed out my suspension, and I carried on, at seventy miles an hour as if nothing had happened. I don't claim to have done anything fancy to keep the bike straight and true, to make sure I landed on both wheels and not the front one - it just happened.

And I rode on, slower now, realising that I had just had a very lucky escape. Realising that I could be dead.

Once again, that night in the bar, one of the Belgian drivers said he and his co-driver had seen me hit the dune. They were a little way behind and told me that they could see in the sand where I took off and, somewhat further on, where I landed and that I'd travelled about twenty metres through the air.

And as I rode on into the afternoon, knowing I had had two close calls, thoughts of mortality naturally began to play around in my head. Of *course* I was going too fast. Of *course* I should have been riding slowly across this unknown *piste*, picking my way carefully in case something unseen and unnoticed were to throw me down. But how boring. I concluded that, given the choice, I would much rather die in a motorcycle accident speeding across the desert in a totally irresponsible manner than wither away by degrees, eking out a mundane existence in the grey world of sensible living...

As the sun began to sink low on the horizon, the wind stilled and the air became crisp and clear under a dark blue sky. We left the wide, dry riverbed we'd been following all day and began to head up into a range of low, rounded hills. Every so often we came across strange piles of sand, about three feet high, that had been dug out of the desert surface. At one of our rest stops I asked the driver of the guide 4X4 what they were. He told me they were the cairns marking the Pari-Dakar route from a few years back. We had been following these cairns for a number of miles and continued to follow them for another hour. He wrote what looked like some numbers on the dust-covered door of the Ford the years this track had been used: it looked like '98 and '06, but I can't be sure.

While we were resting, he pointed to a ridge of hills about three miles away to the east, on the crest of which were some tall aerials: "Military," he informed us. "Morocco military." Then he drew lines in the sand and showed us another line of hills: "Algerian military," he said, then pointed to the space between the two and made signs and noises to indicate explosions.

"Mines?" Gareth asked and he nodded.

This whole southern border between Morocco and Algeria is mined, as is the border between Morocco and Mauritania. The problem is that very little record of just *where* the mines were laid have been kept so it's best to keep well away. This is especially so across the border between Morocco and Mauritania where the whole area has been repeatedly mined by various belligerent forces but no one knows where any of the mines are. He instructed us to ride directly behind him and in line with the Cruisers until we reached Foum-Zguid because the military would be watching us and would not be happy if we strayed away from the track. Needless to say, we did so.

After a brief rest, we made our way through these smooth-sided hills and then dropped into a strange valley where grass and green acacia trees were growing in such profusion that it looked like Southern African savannah. Through this section a maze of tracks divided and joined so that our guide had to turn us back a few times when he missed his way. At one time we saw the driver and the guide involved in a heated argument over which was the correct route. Just how Gareth and I were supposed to have found our way across over one hundred miles of this varied desert landscape when the local Bedouin guide lost his way a number of times makes me shudder to think.

As the sun was setting, we paused to top up our petrol tanks and then continued on, riding into the sun, feeling the air cool against our skin as the shadows lengthened and colour leached from the land. The long ranges of mountains on either side of us turned lilac, then purple and then black when, in the distance across a wide, featureless *reg*, we saw lights twinkling at the base of a high range of mountains - it was Foum-Zguid. Although seemingly so close, it took us another half an hour to cross the *reg* before we reached its outskirts and made our way, in convoy with the Belgians, to their hotel where we booked in too, well pleased with our day's adventure.

Sadly, this amazing day was spoiled by the Tuareg guide, who wanted us to pay him for taking us across. I - reasonably and logically, I thought - explained that we had already paid his friend who had only taken us thirteen miles and that he should ask him for a share of our payment. He wouldn't accept this and became unpleasant but I dug my heels in and refused. We'd been scammed once and I wasn't prepared to lie down and be the compliant foreigner.

After a hot shower, we joined the Belgians in the bar and spent a pleasant hour sharing anecdotes about the day.

Six mad Frenchmen

Both Gareth and I agreed that if we were to head home now, we would feel more than satisfied with what we had achieved and experienced on this trip. But, although we didn't know it then, there were five high points on the trip and we had, so far, only experienced two. The third was about to meet up with us within hours in the shape of six mad Frenchmen.

Both we and the bikes had taken a bit of a battering over the past few days, so we decided that all four of us needed a long, gentle rest day heading south.

That was the plan.

I was looking forward to some stress-free riding, a gathering of reserves before we attempted the next *piste*.

But on trips like these, plans have a tendency to be shouldered aside by circumstance - like meeting a bunch of Russian bikers the previous year off on a jolly to Severodvinsk and being invited to join them.

So, washed, fed and rested we set off on a good tar road making for Tata, Akka and, ultimately, Bouizaka with the aim of later exploring one of the longer *pistes* across the flatter desert regions of southern Morocco close to the Mauritanian and Algerian borders. But within hours of setting off, we passed a garage and café, outside of which were parked some strange-looking contraptions. Of course, we had to investigate so pulled over and had a sniff around. They were three motorcycle-sidecar outfits, but not the conventional ones you would see on the road. These were lightweight, specially constructed for sidecar-cross racing or long-distance, off-road travel. Each had obviously been hand crafted and they looked as if they'd just been stolen from off the set of a Mad Max movie. With them was another Frenchman riding a KTM300 trail bike and two 4X4 backup vehicles. We then remembered that this group had passed us going the other way when we were headed for Zagora and our first desert *piste*.

The Frenchmen were standing around drinking coffee; they looked tired and trail-worn. As always when a bunch of dusty motorcycle travellers happen upon one another on the road, we got talking (and, as usual, we spoke English and they spoke, well, broken English). And, after a short time chatting and sharing our experiences, where we had been and where we were going, they asked whether we'd like to join them. They were a loosely cohesive group of mostly outfit riders who liked extreme challenges; they embark upon one long trip a year, alternating between Africa and Europe (where, for some strange reason, they revelled in travelling in sub-zero conditions just for the hell of it). They had hired an interesting man - Bruno, a paraplegic - as a guide and organiser who was backing them up with two 4X4s, drivers and a mechanic and they were about to head into the mountains following some obscure tracks for the next two days. They would be *bivouacking* - their word - in the mountains that night and did we have food, tents etc?

We did and we would.

There was no need for Gareth and me to consult: Of *course* we would join them. If tagging along with them would be anything like the time we spent with the Russian Black Bears, we were in!

Later that night, Gareth mentioned something that meant a lot to me. He said that these hardy Frenchmen must have seen something in us that made them comfortable inviting us along. When you are a closely-knit bunch of guys on your annual expedition, having paid a great deal of money to employ guides and back-up vehicles, you don't just invite any old bikers you meet outside a café on the side of the road to join you in the mountains for two days. As I mentioned about our joining the Belgians in their Land Cruisers, once you become part of a group and set off into remote places, you become responsible for each other. These Frenchmen must have known that if we had broken down or found that, half way up into the mountains one of us - me, the old man - couldn't cope, they would be responsible for getting us through. So, in their eyes, we obviously looked capable of coping with what they were about to attempt and they felt they would like to spend time with us. That sort of trust made us both feel very special.

So, while the Frenchmen finished their coffee, we topped up our tanks, filled our petrol and water containers, bought some food and were ready to join them when they set off, heading for the beginning of the *piste* they were going to follow - about twenty miles up the road from Tissnt (the silly side of me immediately wants to say, "'Tis.. Tissnt... Tis!'") across the mountains to Taliouine in the north.

So much for our restful day's riding. Yesterday it was sand, today rocks.

As with our seven-hour trip across the desert, I find it very difficult to find the words adequately to describe that day's ride. With one 4X4 in front and one at the back, the Frenchman on the KTM ranging about whenever we crossed a wide, rocky riverbed, looking for the track again on the other side, we rode up and up through desolate mountain valleys, usually following dry riverbeds along tracks cut out of the sides of the mountains;

these tracks must have crossed the dry, rocky beds of rivers at least twenty times. Sometimes, when we lost our way, we would have to ride over boulders up the riverbed, looking for signs of the track. Again my bash plate took a hammering as, heavily laden, I bounced and slithered over rocks the size of footballs that littered the riverbeds.

We stopped for a lunch break in a patch of sandy desert where a grove of palms grew alongside a pool of water. In the still air it was oppressively hot and our oranges were a godsend. Up to now the Frenchmen had kept pretty much to themselves, and we didn't intrude or presume to share their food or space. It was clear they were happy to have us along but they weren't matey; part of the reason for this, I feel, was that we spoke no French and their English was hesitant at best.

After an hour's rest, we set off again, riding through the mountains for the rest of the day. Occasionally we passed through small villages whose square, rock-built houses seemed to extrude from the steep mountain sides into which they had been built; if we stopped near any habitation, the faint sound of dogs, children playing, cocks crowing came to us from far away, carried on the still mountain air. The riverbeds were dry but there were signs that, when in flood, torrents of water would race down these narrow valleys carrying massive boulders with the flow.

In the late afternoon we stopped next to the dry, sandy bed of a small *oed* and set up camp. Bruno looked at the sky and told us that it was safe to put up our tents in the riverbed because no rain was forecast. While Bruno's drivers erected a large communal sleeping tent for the Frenchmen, the outfit riders started pulling their outfits apart, doing maintenance and repairs. They carried trunks of tools and spares in the two 4X4 support vehicles which they dragged out and opened next to their dismembered outfits.

If I had to do an arduous trip across forbidding terrain, far from garages or help, these are the kind of bikers I'd be happy to travel with. While the spaghetti was being cooked in a massive aluminium pot, one outfit rider, Perrick Vendé, got down to work and replaced his bike's worn rear tyre with a brand new knobbly, then replaced his chain and the sidecar's shock absorber. Stripped to the waist, long, matted hair hanging in his face, he worked with a studied efficiency that spoke of long hours building and maintaining his beloved machine. The replacement shock absorber didn't fit, though - there was a piece of aluminium jutting out that got in the way of the frame, so Perrick jacked up the rear wheel of the outfit, started the engine and used the edge of the spinning chain as a Heath Robinson-ish grinder, wearing down the protruding aluminium stub until the shock absorber fitted.

Problem solved.

It was obvious that, if need be, they'd be able to strip their bikes and the sidecars down to the last nut and bolt and put them back together again, gearbox and all. Gareth was totally amazed when he was shown a metal scraper (like the ones you use for scraping paint off walls) that had a rectangular piece of metal cut out of the blade. A few days before, the KTM had died on the side of the road. They quickly discovered the problem: the reed valve was shot. So they cut a piece of metal from this scraper, fitted it in place of the reed valve and the bike worked perfectly for the rest of the trip (except for burning out a plug the next day and getting lost for three hours).

Slowly we began to integrate with these hardy, rough but most likable Frenchmen. Gareth was doing some maintenance on his KTM off to one side where we had pitched our tents and had left some bolts resting on his seat. One of the Frenchmen needed a similar bolt for a repair on his bike and, amongst much laughter, crept up behind Gareth as if to steal one. But Gareth had a set of spare bolts in his toolkit and was able to give them one. *Quid pro quo.* The ice was further broken when they insisted we share some of their spaghetti; my contribution was what was left of our salami (I didn't tell them that I'd saved it from the cats) and they were most appreciative. Evidently they'd been dining on nothing but spaghetti and tomato for days and it was beginning to pall. We sat down just outside their circle, not wanting to presume to join them without an invitation but they offered us some wine and we were quickly drawn into their close-knit group.

As the evening progressed, we all sat together around a gas lantern on jerry cans and tin trunks and spare wheels, they talking animatedly amongst themselves about the day (I assume) while we sat, part of the group, absorbed into their camaraderie. Later, under a crisp star-lit sky, one of them brought out a bottle of Sake that was passed round until it was finished; then out came some whiskey in a nondescript plastic bottle. This too was passed round. Who would drink the last few mouthfuls was decided when one of the Frenchmen smoothed out a piece of sand between our feet and spun an empty wine bottle amidst a great deal of laughter and cheering.

It was a very male time. There was a sense of bonding which was quite palpable. They told us that for these trips their "club" had only one rule: Any one can bring a woman along on one condition: They pay for *all* the petrol during the trip.

I thought that was sensitively done - not: *No women allowed*, but: Of *course* you can bring a woman - just pay for all the petrol...

These guys were all hard-core bikers who lived for their sport, lavished attention on their machines and really knew what they were doing. Riding an outfit in good conditions is difficult enough; riding up these rocky tracks with hairpin bends, through soft sand, across boulder-strewn river beds is something else entirely. Just how good they were was demonstrated the next day when we finally reached a clearer track and we left the 4X4s behind; I was riding as fast as my loaded bike would safely take along this rocky track with its sharp turns and many steep descents into narrow creeks - and the outfit riders were staying with us all the way.

The pillion riders must have had balls the size of grapefruit because there was no way in the world I would stand on the sidecar, clinging onto a curved piece of pipe attached across the front of the sidecar and flinging myself from one side to the other to balance the bike round turns. These pillion riders were incredibly tough. Their hands looked almost unnatural, like they were wearing a pair of fleshy boxing gloves over their normal hands; the muscles and tendons in their arms were like wires and bicycle tubes under the skin. Despite this strength, when I offered the salami and a knife to one of the pillion riders that night, he showed me his hands - which were swollen and stiff so that the fingers could hardly move - and asked me to cut some off for him; his hands just didn't work after a day's clinging on to the outfit.

Their main guide and organiser, Bruno, a Frenchman living permanently in Morocco, was an intriguing man. He spent his time either in the passenger seat of one of the 4X4s or in his stripped down wheelchair, as personalised and utilitarian as the outfits he was leading, with quick-release wheels and so light he could wheel himself with relative ease across rocks and sand. His face was ascetic, thin and darkly tanned, his nose aquiline, shoulder-length grey hair tucked into a worn baseball cap, gold ear ring in each ear, greying stubble, dark glasses tucked into his cap. His useless legs, thin and stick-like under his jeans, perched on the footrests of his wheelchair; utility vest containing various bits and pieces he would need during the day loosely over his chest; worn, faded and patched jeans, canvas rucksack strapped behind the wheel chair holding his urine bottle, water and other basics. No one treated him like an invalid; there were times when he needed help - like getting into the 4X4 or if he found himself trapped in his wheelchair amongst large rocks - and someone would unobtrusively give him a hand. He negotiated soft sand and rocks by adroitly lifting the front wheels of his chair and pushing himself along, balancing on the main wheels, with a grim but friendly independence respected by the French bikers around him. Despite his apparent handicap, he was very involved in rallying and was a member of an international rally co-ordinating committee and gave advice on routes in Morocco including sections of the Pari-Dakar.

What impressed me so much about him was his independence, his spirit, his *normality* despite the fact that he had lost the use of both his legs.

We all have much to learn from people like that. (Although tempted, I won't start ranting about people who abuse the benefit system...)

One of the Frenchmen used to compete in side-car cross in the early days using Norton Commando engines - they gave the best weight to power ratio at the time, he told us. With a wry smile he added that they also destroyed many engines. Two years ago, just a week before they were to set off on one of their trips to Morocco, an electrical short set fire to his bike and burned it out completely. A friend offered to lend him his BMW1000 which he adapted to take his outfit. He said it went so well that he bought another BMW for this trip. His normal bike is a KTM990, like Gareth's. He admitted that he's also dropped it a few times in sand and smiled at the thought of picking it up. Gareth empathised - in just one day he had developed blisters on his hands from keeping control of his heavy bike over the boulders.

A lost rider and entertaining children

The next morning, before the sun was fully up, some of the Frenchmen were already working on their bikes, getting them ready for the day. We set off after breakfast on another day riding through the mountains.

About midday, we came across a large village almost hidden in a deep cleft in the mountains, the houses made out of the same rocks into which they were nestled so that, from a distance, they blended in and seemed to become part of the cliff face itself. In the valley floor grew thousands of palms, their dusty olive green fronds shrouding the road in places so that we seemed to be riding through a shaded tunnel between the mountains. We rested there for a while, walking into the dense thicket of palms and seeing the intricate network of small canals leading water to their fields, bright green with new wheat, all with raised earthen borders to contain the water. Women in brightly coloured *djellabas* worked the fields - purple and lilac, red, orange, yellow - so bright they looked like iridescent beetles against the background of dun earth and dark rocks, gentle-faced women who eyed us shyly as we passed, slim-bodied and sleek of skin like whippets.

As I said, there are no fat people in Morocco.

Then the track climbed up the side of the valley, a narrow ledge of road cut from the rock that zig-zagged its way up to above fifteen hundred metres onto a high, wind-swept plateau. It was intensely beautiful and, when we looked down on the village from near the top, seeing the splash of green from the palms in amongst the rocks, the small rectangular stone houses, I had to pause quietly and absorb it, *will* my mind to take and hold it like a snapshot. The mountain road rivalled Sani Pass, which claws its way up the Drakensberg Mountains between Natal and Lesotho. This was wilder, more remote, a wonderful road hidden in the mountains.

Making our way down into another valley, we realised that we had lost the KTM rider who often roared off ahead on his own, exploring. We paused in the sand of the dry riverbed and waited.

And waited...

Some of the outfit riders headed back the way we had come, looking for side tracks he might have taken by mistake; others rode on ahead to look for him, checking in the dust for his tracks. After a while they returned - nothing.

The one 4X4 driver/mechanic settled down to do some maintenance: petrol was leaking from a small hole in the tank and his prop-shaft was leaking oil from the transfer box. He lay under the truck, removed the prop-shaft and repacked the oil seal. There was nothing he could do with the tank so he left it to drip quietly into the sand.

While he worked on the truck, I went for a walk down the riverbed, the rocks glinting with flecks of mica and silica in the harsh sunlight. Far from the vehicles and surrounded by a tumble of huge rocks, I came across a still pool of water which had seeped from under the sand, surrounded by stunted palms; the water was icy cold as it emerged from underground and I bent to drink. Sheltered from the others by the rocks that surrounded me, I was overcome by a feeling of solitude, alone in a small oasis deep in the mountains. In amongst the rocks, I was drawn by a tiny, bright splash of colour. And there, clinging to life, was a small plant that had somehow found the energy to produce one yellow flower.

It made me think of the women in their colourful *djellabas*, living their lives so exuberantly in this seeming wilderness.

Back at the vehicles, there was still no sign of the KTM rider. The mechanic had sorted the prop-shaft so we packed up and headed on until we reached the next village where again we stopped and waited for over an hour.

During this time, as always happens, we were surrounded first by little boys who clustered around the bikes touching things; they climbed onto the sidecars at Perrick's invitation, and were allowed to rev the engines, much to their delight. A small group of girls, veils covering their heads like young Madonnas, held back, smiling shyly but turning away warily if we approached them, like wild deer anxious at the unexpected proximity of a human. But slowly, as the afternoon waned, they inched closer until, quickly snapping a picture, I managed to coax them to look at the photograph. All anxiety and suspicion gone, they clustered around, giggling at the image of themselves captured on the screen.

Still we waited. The KTM rider still hadn't turned up nor could any of the French riders find him. It had been over three hours now.

I was sitting alone a short way from the others when two girls, about 16, approached me. Heads loosely draped with their *djellabas* that blew in the wind, they held them in place with gestures delicate and fine. For a moment I thought they would walk past but they stopped and greeted me. This was most unusual - usually Moroccan women stay well clear of strangers (and particularly male strangers) - but they were quite relaxed in my presence. We tried to communicate but it was impossible. Even hand gestures were misunderstood and they laughed at my earnest attempts at sign language. In the end, we exchanged names - one was called Gabela, I remember - and touched hands briefly in greeting. I was honoured that they had felt confident enough to approach me and were relaxed in my presence.

Back at the bikes, Perrick was entertaining a crowd of giggling boys, teaching them to sing:

"Alouette, gentille alouette,

Alouette, je te plumerai ..."

- followed by a spirited rendition of *"I like to move it move it!"* with matching actions, much to their delight. Then he filled his mouth with water and chased them screaming around the dusty village square.

A silent group of adults gathered on one side and watched, smiling. They did not approach us.

Later some of the Frenchmen set off again to look for the lost rider and, this time, they found him. He had taken a wrong turning a while back and then broken down. They managed to load the bike into the back of a passing van and it was taken to our hotel later that night. (They repaired it the next morning - burned-out spark plug.)

Finally off again, we left the 4X4s behind and all rode fast across a *hamada* - a vast high plateaux - forty to fifty miles an hour along a rocky, undulating track, snow-capped mountains in the distance, until we reached the main road again.

That evening during our meal, Perrick asked us whether we would like to ride with them for another day. They were heading north, following a similar *piste* higher into the mountains up to four thousand metres. We asked Bruno, the organiser and guide, if he was OK with us staying with them.

He agreed - "No problem."

Then one of the other Frenchmen, usually silent and very reserved, said to us in faltering English, "It has been a pleasure to have you with us."

A very special moment.

At some time in the evening - whether it was alcohol induced, I'm not sure, but Vincent, one of the Frenchmen, bald-headed, quiet and immensely strong, turned to us and, with a smile (probably because he knew we wouldn't be able to do it) said he wanted us to have a go riding his outfit for a bit the next day. Both his invitation for us to stay with them on their final *piste* and his offer of a ride on his precious machine were real evidence that we had been accepted as one of them - honorary Frenchmen, in a way. Vincent, we discovered from Perrick, is a seven-time Paris-Dakar entrant but never once did he mention it. Evidently, he was the first to ride an outfit in the Dakar rally.

Sadly, when we woke the next morning it was raining and Bruno informed us that would be too dangerous to head into the mountains because the rivers would be high. It was not to be.

That is my one real regret of the trip - that we missed out on spending one more day in the remote High Atlas Mountains with this great bunch of Frenchmen, that we hadn't had a chance to ride one of their outfits. They had given us lasting memories - and what a privilege it had been getting to know and riding with them.

So we parted company in the rain: they making their way to Marrakech and then home; we heading south to attempt one of the very long *pistes* near the Algerian/Mauritanian borders.

South to Laayoune and a slight contretemps with a policeman

We took the tar road towards Agadair through light rain, heading for the coast. At Tiznit we stopped for lunch; as usual, we found a small, smoky place that caters solely for locals and ordered a plate of stuff bubbling away in a pot (there was no menu - you took pot luck - literally). Plates of greyish legumes and bits of meat, that we soon realised were sheep's intestines cut up into ragged chunks, were placed on the plastic table in front of us. (There were also some crunchy bits but I didn't want to look too closely. Probably wind-pipe cartilage.) We both agreed that, perhaps, we had gone too "local" this time when the after taste of the offal lingered rather unpleasantly for the rest of the day.

From Tisnit we took a small picturesque road over a low range of mountains to the coast. A cold wind blowing off the Atlantic up the western slopes brought the rain again but by the time we reached the sea it had dried. A delightful fast winding road lead us to Sidi Infi and we booked into a cheap hotel overlooking the beach, so close we were able to watch some surfers from our first floor window.

That evening we met a bunch of Polish bikers riding KTM990s supported by two 4X4s who'd done a lot of travelling around

Morocco, covering similar *pistes* as we had. One wanted to join us on our trip south and into the desert and commented how frustrating it was when you meet good people - I assume he meant us - to ride with when on the road but struggle to get people to join you from the start.

The next day we were up early, making our way back over the coastal mountain range, green and wet from the relief rain blowing in from the Atlantic, then at Guelim we turned south for the long ride down the coast to Laayoune, a town I remember well from the Plymouth-Dakar Old Bangers Challenge I had participated in a number of years before. We had travelled down this long coastal road - a column of weirdly decorated old bangers, heading for Mauritania, Senegal and The Gambia. It was good to be here again, just the two of us this time. At first, we rode across a flat valley between two long, low ranges of rounded mountains before turning abruptly west at Tan Tan and making for the coast. (Tan Tan, according to Julian Noel, the inspiration behind the Plymouth-Dakar Old Bangers Challenges, "... is a town so ugly they had to name it twice.")

The landscape became progressively desert-like as we continued south, the vegetation thinning until only foot-high scrubby plants, mostly covered in thorns, could cling onto life, then these too disappeared and we followed the beautiful soft curves of some high Sief dunes, the ones on the right a pale yellow, almost white, while the ones to our left, further away, were a deeper yellow - a trick of the light, I am sure. The sheep had long disappeared, then it was the goats and, finally, only the occasional camel could be seen, staring contemptuously into the middle distance, contemplating the aeons that had passed by in this desolate landscape. The light became brighter, reflecting off the sand until it hurt the eyes; clouds disappeared and all colour seemed to drain out of the landscape. For one hundred and fifty miles we rode close to the sea cliff, sometimes just twenty metres away, spray from the Atlantic waves occasionally bursting above the cliffs as we rode. Lone fishermen sat stoically on the crumbling cliff edge, waiting for a bite. Their small shelters made from stones, mud and plastic bags fluttering in the wind spoke eloquently of their struggle for survival in this barren land.

Just before Tan Tan we crossed the mouth of the Oed Draa as it entered the sea, a pathetic remnant of the vast watercourse that stretches east and south for seven hundred miles from the High Atlas, flowing across the desert until it finally reaches the coast, forming most of the Algerian-Moroccan frontier. In places it is over sixty miles wide and yet, by the time it reaches the sea, most of its water has evaporated or sunk back into the desert sand, leaving a small, shallow trickle, a pathetic remnant of its vast water-cut expanse that so dominates the interior of Morocco.

Now that we were further south (and closer to the troubled Algerian/Mauritanian borders) at the entrance to every town we were met by police who pulled us over, asked for our *fiches* and passports and then requested additional information, seemingly at random, like our telephone numbers in England, our occupations and so on. They were invariably pleasant and friendly (except for one with whom we had a slight *contrempts* later) but, after a while, we found the constant scrutiny, the time wasted while our documents were methodically checked, most annoying.

Finally, tired and hot after riding across three hundred and forty miles of seemingly endless nothingness, we reached the outskirts of Laayune.

Another police check-point.

We handed over our documents, went through the usual rigmarole, answered all the questions and then were waved on. Twenty metres further down the road was *another* police checkpoint - and we naturally assumed that they were all together, part of the same contingent, and blithely rode through.

(Why would the same people - us - be stopped to have the same documents scrutinized by police who stood on the side of the road within shouting distance of each other? I ask with a certain logical reasonableness.)

Within seconds we were alerted to our mistake by angry hooting from the parked police car and a furious man in uniform waving at us to return forthwith. We hastily u-turned and pulled up alongside a nasty spiked Stinger contraption waiting to be deployed in case any motorist tried to make a run for it. A very angry man strode up to us, demanding why we hadn't stopped.

It was difficult to say, "Look, you stupid fellow, when you've just spent a quarter of an hour giving all your details to one group of policemen, a normal person would assume that he wouldn't have to stop and do it all again within twenty metres, wouldn't he? Why don't you get together and *share* the information then you wouldn't have to hassle us twice?" but I felt it wiser just to hold out my hands in grovelling apology, point to the two groups of police just metres apart and say, "Sorry, we thought you were together."

Again and again he demanded why we hadn't stopped and all I could do was apologise and repeat, "Sorry, we thought you were together."

Then I realised what was happening. He had deliberately placed himself between us and his colleagues, his face taking on that unmistakably sly look, the lowered voice, "Mmmmm, this serious. You don't stop... serious. What can we do? Mmmmm?"

I apologised again and looked blank, waiting for the request for money.

"Mmmmmm," he repeated, frowning. "This serious. You don't stop. Mmmmmm. What we do now?"

"Arrest me?" I suggested, trying to be helpful. I wasn't going to play his little game.

Then, quietly so his fellow officer wouldn't hear, he muttered, "Seventy Euro -"

"And you'll give me a receipt?" I asked reasonably (and loudly), getting off the bike and removing my jacket, letting him know that I was prepared for the long wait.

He realised he wasn't going to get anything out of us and waved us on in a most bad-tempered manner.

I really don't like people who try to bribe me. (Nor does Gareth, as he demonstrated later.)

We rode into town and booked into a ropy hotel that cost all of £5.00 a night for both of us, stripped off our hot riding gear and looked forward to a quiet rest. Within minutes, though, there was a knock on our door and a Moroccan man, late thirties, I would imagine, introduced himself as Sayid, proud owner of an Africa Twin and self-appointed chairman of the local motorcycle club. He invited us to join him for a cup of coffee and listen to him talk about himself. (Well, he didn't actually say that, but that's what happened.)

As soon the coffee arrived he got out his mobile phone: "Look! That's a picture of me and my Africa Twin. That's a picture of me ... Another picture of me ... Me going across the river - look at the mud on my tyres! A picture of me ... Look, here is a video of me riding in the desert. The man taking the video is driving on a tar road and - look! I'm going faster than him! A picture of me... Look at all the fish I caught... Me and my Africa Twin... Me... Look, me riding my Africa Twin in the desert..."

I think he showed us every photo and video on his phone. After twenty minutes of this I got bored; Gareth had more manners and continued to feign interest.

"Where are you eating?" he asked, realising he had run out of pictures to show us. He had a friend (where had we heard this before?) who owned a fish restaurant. He would come and fetch us. We could eat together.

I know it sounds churlish, but, once again, we had been latched onto by a polite but garrulous man who seemed to do little more than talk. And after a long, hard day's ride, all I want to do is rest and relax, have a wash, read a little and then quietly walk about the town, absorbing the sights and sounds and smells peculiar to the place. Sitting listening to a man talk about himself mindlessly for hours is not what I need. He took us outside to have a look at his Africa Twin and Gareth had to fend him off taking a ride on his KTM. In the end he - Gareth - lied and said that he wouldn't even let his *father* - pointing at me while I looked suitably crestfallen - ride his beloved bike and that seemed to silence him.

Later that evening he led us through the town of Laayune to his friend's huge, airy restaurant where we were fed salad and a fish platter that ended up costing us five times what we paid for our hotel room.

Throughout the meal Sayid talked. He didn't stop. Afterwards Gareth and I were not sure whether he was interested in us, intent on practicing his English, trying to convert us to Islam or making contacts to set up a motorcycle touring company with the lure of a desert rally. He instructed us on the malicious effects of smoking, explaining in great detail, as if to children, on how each of the six poisons - his statistic - in cigarettes damages the body. He told us why Moslems don't drink alcohol and explained in detail the deleterious effects of alcohol on the system, both physical and moral. He tried to convince us to log on to the website of a Moslem immam who broadcast in English over the Internet, repeatedly mentioning the web address and telling us how important it was that we listened to him. He informed how well, as a Moslem, he looked after his parents and in-laws, quoting from the Koran to back up his views. He explained to us that there were more oil reserves under the soil of Morocco than in the whole of the Emirates; that America, France, Germany and Algeria were conspiring against Morocco to control the oil supply but that their king was playing a long game, waiting for the oil in the Middle East to run out before releasing Moroccan oil onto the market. He wanted us to bring British bikers to Laayune, promising to organise a rally - he had government backing, he assured us - and there would be TV coverage...

While he was lecturing us, I surreptitiously fed much of the rather tasteless leftover fish to a hungry cat lurking under my chair who instantly became my friend.

The next morning, before we were able to pack up and leave, he was there again, knocking on our door, inviting us to visit him at his office (a Moroccan oil company) for coffee and more of the same talk.

We loaded up the bikes and, reluctantly, made our way to the building. Outside the office door stood two uniformed guards. Inside, women sat idly at empty desks. In his office, Sayid sat behind his large executive desk, still dressed - for some reason - in his motorcycle leathers. He ordered coffee. A minion brought it.

He talked. We drank our coffee.

No phone rang, no one entered or left the building, no papers were signed, no work was being done.

Very much an African office.

Eventually we managed to prize ourselves away. As we left, he was trying to persuade us to stay another night, sleep at his beach house, shoot rabbits in the desert with him; he had never ridden the *piste* we were about to attempt and perhaps he could join us...

If he had ridden with us into the desert, I believe I would have had to kill him.

On the street outside, an old Land Cruiser drove past with *five* camels packed, nose to tail like pencils in a box, on the back. How on earth do you get five camels onto the back of a Land Cruiser? How do you ask them to shuffle up a little, make room?

It made me think of the elephant jokes from my youth: How do you get an elephant into a matchbox? - *Take the matches out...*

These Sahara people don't know the law

The policeman at the checkpoint just before we headed east out of Laayune asked, "Destination?"

Gareth replied, "El-Samara."

The policeman looked surprised. "What do you want to go to Samara for? It's got *nothing* - no animals, no trees, no houses, nothing - only desert. Mmmm - a teacher and a engineer in the desert."

We headed out on a good tar road and I thought to myself: That's as apt a description as any I can think of to summarise our trip - *A teacher and an engineer in the desert...*

At first there were road signs - just two, spaced twenty miles apart: a warning triangle with a picture of a camel underneath.

Why?

As I rode, I imagined a Moroccan Roads Department planning meeting, guards at the door, people sitting at desks doing nothing. In a cool, darkened office, a man dressed still in his motorbike leathers addresses his fellow planners after inviting them to his friend's restaurant for lunch:

"There are no signs on this road here. If we are to be a modern country, we must have signs on our roads."

"You are right, my friend. What signs should we have?"

"We should have some signs warning drivers about something. That's what roads signs are for - they are to warn people."

"What must we warn people about?"

They pause, deep in thought.

"How about camels?"

"Yes, camels is good. We will put two signs."

"With warning triangles."

"Yes, with warning triangles. So that they know they are being warned."

"I have a friend who makes signs ... "

We passed the carcases of many destroyed and abandoned tyres left on the roadside. The landscape became more desolate. There were almost no cars on the road. No people, no houses, no animals (I lie - there was one donkey, I remember it distinctly) - just a flat land broken briefly by a few stunted trees and rocks; then the plants disappeared; then most of the rocks, leaving a featureless expanse of *reg* as far as the eye could see.

We reached Simara by mid-day and stopped at a café to drink something cool. It was getting so hot during the day now that we seldom felt like eating. We bought bread to eat with the tins of fish I had been able to buy the previous day so we had enough food for two days, filled up our water containers including some extra bottles, twelve litres in total, filled our tanks and all our spare containers (an extra seventeen litres) and set off only to be stopped yet again on the outskirts of town by the police.

After the usual protracted questions and checks, we waited in the heat while they radioed the police in Laayune to verify our story. I pictured an underground bunker where uniformed men stood over a map, little plastic motorbikes attached to blocks of wood being moved by a woman pushing a stick, tracking us right across Morocco:

The British motorcyclists have reached Simara.

Check.

What is their destination?

They say they are going into the desert.

Why do they do that? There is nothing there...

While we were waiting, a battered Series 2 Land Rover pulled up at the checkpoint. A loud altercation began between one of the policemen and an old Moroccan man in faded traditional dress, face burned mahogany brown from the sun. Eventually, after much shouting and gesticulating, the old man climbed back into his Land Rover and drove away, trailing blue smoke.

The policeman walked up to us and said apologetically, "These Sahara people don't know the law."

Sahara people.

Yes, I thought to myself - we are in the Sahara.

I must admit that, as we set off towards Tan Tan and the turnoff to the east which would take us four hundred miles into the desert, I felt both excited and apprehensive. After the first two hundred miles, we would be following a *piste* that Gareth had marked with waypoints every twenty miles or so on his GPS. Part of this *piste* was supposed to follow an old Pari-Dakar route, marked with cairns every five hundred metres but, although we didn't know it then as we set out, we were never able to find this track.

This desert is frighteningly large, very empty and desolate; and the four hundred miles we were about to attempt over the next two days was an unknown. The map indicated that the first part of the route was a "road under construction" and so it proved to be. In fact, the first seventy-odd miles were good tar and we made quick progress. I had mixed feelings about this: relieved in a way that we were not battling our way through soft sand but disappointed because we hadn't come all this way to ride along a tar road across the desert. But despite the tar that gave the landscape a semblance of civilization, in that first seventy miles we saw no human beings at all. Nothing - not a car, pedestrian, village or even a donkey. The road just made its lonely way across flat featureless desert, slightly stony with the occasional hardy, scrubby bushes, long ranges of dark hills in the distance. No dunes, no soft sand.

Then, after seventy three miles, we came across our first vehicle, our first human - an old Arab man in a battered Series 3 Land Rover. He drove past without acknowledging us, heading in the opposite direction. It seemed as if, to him, we were an inconsequential aberration in this place, irrelevant transients not even worth a sideways glance as he made his stoical way to somewhere in this vast expanse of nothingness...

A Boy's Own adventure

A few miles further on, the tar ended and we made our way through an area churned up, I assume, by graders and trucks, the proposed road continuing ahead of us in various stages of completion. But there were no vehicles or construction crew working the road. A grader had obviously laboured its way across the desert marking the path of the new road, cutting a track as wide as its blade through the stony surface and we followed this - although Gareth became concerned as we headed further and further to the east, away from the waypoints marked on his GPS.

What to do? Should we keep on following this clearly-demarcated track or head off west into the desert and try to strike the smaller *piste*, the old Pari-Dakar track supposedly marked with cairns that we had obviously missed?

In retrospect, having travelled right across this section of desert until we reached the main north-south road, we should have looked for the track. One of our great disappointments on this trip was that we missed this *piste* and the old Pari-Dakar route. Both Gareth and I would dearly love to return and complete it, perhaps venture even further into the desert, because the fearful unknown that we felt then is now gone; we now know what the desert surface in the far southern part of Morocco is like and feel confident that we could navigate through it just following a compass bearing. There is very little soft sand, the surface flat and reasonably firm, easy to cross.

But things always look easier in retrospect.

At the time we were concerned. We just didn't know what to expect, whether there were vast sections of soft sand to negotiate, steep-sided canyons or rivers to cross. In the end, the clear track ploughed by the bulldozer was more comforting than the frightening thought of heading off across trackless desert looking for a *piste* we didn't even know existed in any greater reality than random marks on Gareth's GPS, downloaded from a stray website on the Internet.

So we just pressed on, the digital waypoints moving further and further away from us in the ether.

Then our hearts sank as the track we were following began to fade. We still had about 180 miles of desert to cross.

We stopped, a little fearful now.

We poured over the map.

Gareth checked his GPS.

Neither of us wanted to make the decision - press on (there still was a rough track made by the grader using its ripper to cut into the soil but we didn't know how far it would lead before it, too, disappeared into the sand). We were now a long way away from the marked waypoints. We knew we had enough fuel to turn around and make it back, but that was an option we really didn't want to consider.

In the distance we saw a grader with two workers standing on the side of a churned-up piece of track, the first sign of human life we had come across in a long time. We rode up to them and showed them the map. They spoke no English at all. The one kept pointing into the desert at right angles to the direction we were travelling and repeating what we assumed was the name of a village. We thought he was telling us to ride into a vast area of nothingness in the direction of Algeria; using hand gestures he assured us there *was* a *piste* and even took me a few hundred metres into the desert, repeatedly pointing at the ground and into the distance, a featureless stretch of *reg* that disappeared over the horizon.

But I could see nothing, not even faint tyre tracks. Just the desert. A vast, endless, featureless expanse of nothingness stretching into Algeria.

Perhaps the policemen had been right. Why go into the desert - there is nothing there.

Both Gareth and I became even more concerned. We had a number of alternatives, none of which was in any way certain:

First, we could continue straight ahead, hoping the ripped trail left by the grader would continue and lead us all the way through; but it was clear that the construction had come to an end and there was still a very long way to go. What if we continued following the marks only to find they petered out in the middle of nowhere when we had too little fuel to make it back?

Then there was a village marked on the map about eighty miles ahead - Jdiriya - but when we pointed to it and asked whether we could buy petrol there they shook their heads - *Pas d' essence.*

Alternatively, we could head west and try to find the *piste* marked by Gareth's waypoints - about twenty miles diagonally across the desert as the crow flies - and, if we found it, follow that. The concern about this course of action was that Gareth had downloaded the waypoints from off the Internet and had no idea at all whether they would correspond with an actual track along the ground. In fact, right until we reached the main road in mid afternoon the following day, he was apprehensive that we would reach the final waypoint only to find ourselves still in the middle of nowhere with no idea where we were or where to go. I must admit that the thought of just heading off this friendly track - regardless of how faint or tenuous it was - into the desert in the vain hope of stumbling across some *piste* marked with cairns terrified me. I felt like clinging to it as one would clutch onto a lifeline thrown in a storm.

Or, thirdly, we could head off into the desert to the east in the direction the road worker was pointing in the hope we might stumble on a village (and he had told us there was no petrol there, so what would be the point?). The map indicated a village/town called Hawza in the direction we had just come from; we should have ridden through it about twenty miles back but there was nothing there, not even one building, and certainly no fuel. We wondered whether Hawza was a pseudo town like the invented roads on Russian maps that, in reality, just do not exist; or perhaps the track of the new road had by-passed the village.

We just did not know.

We had no definitive information upon which to base a decision and the two road workers we had stumbled upon knew no English.

In the end, the relative safety of the faint tracks disappearing into the distance was the more attractive option and we decided to follow them in the hope they would lead us to Jdiriya - even though there was supposed to be no fuel there. We would make a final decision there.

If we were forced to retrace our steps from Jdiriya, we wouldn't have enough fuel to make it back - but there would be just sufficient for us to reach a tarred road and flag down a vehicle.

As we set off, I must admit to being filled with a sense of apprehension - but not fear. The apprehension was very real: we just didn't know whether we would have enough fuel to make it through and we didn't know whether the track would disappear and leave us lost in the desert. We had no idea whether the terrain would change and become more demanding, perhaps a long section of *erg* we would have to battle our way through.

The lack of actual fear was twofold:

First, I didn't think what we were attempting was life threatening. If one of our bikes had broken down irreparably, or if one of us got injured and couldn't ride, we would still be able to get out on one bike. In an extreme situation, we could mark the exact position of the injured person or damaged bike on the GPS and go for help. And if we got badly lost, we could just keep on heading west and, eventually, we would cut the main Al Mahbas-Zag road and be safe.

Secondly, I was simply very confident in Gareth's ability to get us through (even though, afterwards, he did admit to having some real doubt - although, at the time, he kept it to himself). If I couldn't have Bear Grills or Sir Ranulph Fiennes around, my next choice would be Gareth. His engineering knowledge and ability to repair sick and broken machinery is remarkable; he uses his small, hand-held, second-hand GPS with the expertise of a teenager manipulating a mobile phone. He is always calm, resourceful and controlled. If we were to suffer a serious setback somewhere in this empty desert we had to cross before reaching the main road, I had confidence that he would get us out.

So, in a way, I left the final decision whether to go on or head back to him. If he was up for it, I would go with him. If he felt it too dangerous to make the attempt, I would bow to his wisdom.

But, in reality, neither of us had any desire to turn back.

According to the GPS, Jdiriya was twenty miles ahead of us as the crow flies but turned out to be forty miles across the ground. The track, very rough and stony now, followed a long range of *hamada*, rocky hills to our left for miles before finally turning into them. We entered through a steep-sided valley then made our way up the hills onto a rocky plateau across which we rode for a number of miles. Finally, in the distance ahead of us we could make out a few buildings and an antenna held in place with cables. We made for the closest building, outside of which were three men standing in front of a broken and stripped Land Cruiser - ex-army from the machine-gun mount bolted onto the back. We stopped in front of them and, after exchanging greetings, we asked where we could get fuel.

"Pas d' essence " - followed by a shrug as if to say, "What did you expect?"

Often, in Africa, if you are told there is no fuel and you wait a while, a small child will head off somewhere and spread the message. Shortly thereafter, someone will sidle up and ask you to follow them to a dark hut where a stock of petrol, oil and diesel will be stored in dodgy-looking plastic containers, sold by the bottle at hugely inflated prices. Usually this fuel has been stolen or siphoned from trucks with the driver getting a cut.

But not here. There were no children here, no women, just these three men staring at us.

Gareth unstrapped his spare fuel container and began to top up his tank. I took out my camera and took a photograph.

Bad move.

Suddenly the three men became agitated. They waved their hands in front of me, "No photos! No photos!"

But I had already taken a photo - and they knew it.

Only then did I realise that this was not a town or a village but an army base, a small outpost stuck in the middle of nowhere. The problem was that behind where Gareth was pouring petrol into his tank was this broken-down Land Cruiser. Under the dust I could just see, faintly, camouflage paint. The three men, now that I looked more closely, were wearing odd bits of uniform as well as civilian clothes.

Unsmiling, one approached me and asked to see the picture I had just taken. I was concerned that he was about to confiscate the camera and wondered whether I could remove the memory card without his noticing. He looked closely over my shoulder as I found the picture and showed him, apologising for including the army vehicle in the shot. He peered into the screen, pointed to the trashed Land Cruiser and shook his finger.

Army vehicle. Not allowed.

He made signs indicating that I must delete the picture.

Relieved that he wasn't taking the camera or confiscating my entire memory card, I demonstrated each step: "See - picture ... now, look - delete button ... see, gone, deleted - OK?"

That seemed to satisfy him and tensions relaxed. But - and again this is just *so* Africa - why anyone would object to a photograph of a Land Cruiser that obviously hadn't, by the look of it, been driven anywhere for years is beyond me. If it weren't in the middle of the desert, there'd be weeds growing through the engine block. Unless, Gareth suggested later, they just didn't want the Algerians or any other potential enemy to learn that this lonely military outpost is being manned by three semi-dressed soldiers with access to one scrap-heap of a Land Cruiser to cope with any emergency.

We filled in the usual forms for the soldiers then rode to the next of the three buildings and filled in more forms - this for passport control, I assume. The officer there was most friendly and, when we asked whether we could have some water, gave us two large bottles, ice cold from a fridge somewhere in the building. We both drank deeply and strapped what was left onto our bulging panniers.

With our tanks topped up and sufficient water to last another two days, we were ready to continue on and look for somewhere to camp for the night because by then it was late afternoon. The soldiers had pointed out the direction we ought to go and had drawn a crude map for us in the sand: Here, the track we had entered and, here, a turn off to the left just outside the village/army outpost. We hadn't seen any turnoff when we came in and were concerned that we might miss it but they insisted: Straight then sharp left, pointing over the hills to the west.

Hoping we would not get lost, we set off. Yes, a vague track did branch to the left but it was as if a single car had turned off the road and headed out into the *reg* so the driver could relieve himself, not a *piste* to follow for the next hundred and fifty or so miles across the desert. But Gareth assured me we were heading in the right direction according to his GPS so we pressed on.

And it was about then that we began to gain confidence. As we had learned in our first attempts at crossing a desert *piste,* there never is just *one* track - there are always many and, so long as you keep travelling in vaguely the right direction, you should reach your destination in the end - especially if you are heading for a long road at right angles and not a point. So, with the sun now low on the horizon, we rode on over easy, undulating terrain, looking for somewhere to camp for the night.

Sometimes the track was easy to follow but then, at intervals, it would disappear altogether. But we no longer felt that tightening of the chest: *I'm lost!* We knew that somewhere ahead other tracks would appear. And, anyway, we had our GPSs to keep us heading in the right direction. (Certainly, we both agreed, we would never have attempted this section of desert - or the other *pistes* - without a GPS. We would have become hopelessly lost.)

We found that the tracks were most easy to see when they crossed the side of a hill, catching the late afternoon light, or when we were high up looking out over the flat desert towards the horizon; then the faint tracks became more visible until they disappeared into the distance.

Finally, as the sun began to set, we came across a dry riverbed with a few old, gnarled tamarisk trees to give some focus to an otherwise featureless desert plain, the sand of the riverbed almost pure white, fine-grained and soft. We stripped off to bare torsos because of the heat, set up our tents and collected firewood. Then we indulged in the civilizing luxury of tea.

One hundred and thirty miles to go before we met the north-south road. We would just make it on our petrol with a little to spare.

The sun set over the desert, softening the atmosphere as it always does. We were very far from anywhere.

The air began to cool. We lit the fire and a gentle darkness slowly covered the land. Stars began to emerge from an indigo sky and a low moon appeared on the horizon turning the pale sand of the riverbed strangely bright against the darkness. The desert all about us became hushed and still. Gareth pottered about, taking long exposure photographs while I prepared supper next to the fire.

Stripped away was all the clutter that complicates life and distracts one from the important things: just Gareth and me, father and son, together in the desert. It was like a Boys' Own adventure coming to life. It was something Enid Blighton could have written. And we were *living* it...

All around us was a deep sense of isolation; inside, a feeling of achievement and satisfaction. The bikes were going well; the desert surface we had been travelling across was forgiving but sufficiently challenging and varied to make it interesting. It was the isolation that was the challenge - the realisation that, if we were to break down, we would be in trouble that lent a certain frisson to life.

Two punctures and the Al Mahbas-Zag tar road

The next day we set off early while it was still cool, the sky overcast and grey. And for the next one hundred and thirty miles we rode across the desert in an almost straight line - Gareth showed me the track on his GPS at the end of the day; in fact, you can see it on Google Earth here, in the south:

http://www.hareti.co.uk/php/drawfile.php?file=morocco.txt

Zoom in close and you will see the pale tracks making their way across the desert surface going seemingly nowhere. How I long to go back and ride across them again!

And in those one hundred and thirty miles, which took us six hours to cover, we saw nothing man-made, nothing living except for a falcon that flew over us in the late morning and seemed to pause quizzically and watch us passing below before flying on and disappearing into the deep blue endlessness of the sky that hung silently over us. Even the tracks we followed showed no tyre marks at all, suggesting that the last vehicle had passed this way a long time ago, certainly not since the last rains, and who could tell when those had been? The indentations were there for us to follow, although they forked and converged constantly; at times other tracks suddenly appeared out of the desert at right angles, crossed ours and disappeared with a disturbing purposefulness into the distance until they converged and melded into one another at the limit of sight. Where could they be going? Where had they come from, ruler-straight from horizon to horizon? They were like desert sirens calling us to discover where they led. But we couldn't. We hadn't the time or the fuel to divert from the tracks we were following. Perhaps some other day...

And, although the direction of our travel seldom varied, the colour and texture of the desert did - sometimes it was a pale cream as we crossed a dry riverbed, then a deeper orange, then black stones with yellow sand beneath. When the tacks crossed the bed of an ancient lake, the bikes would hiss along like we were riding on silk, then it would change again as we rode at walking pace over rocky ground, picking our way between the rocks that clanged against my bash plate, making me wince. There were soft, sandy sections too when our wheels would twist and slide a little, but seldom long enough to cause trouble. But, anyway, by now we had become pretty confident riding in soft sand and, so long as we kept up our momentum and controlled the front wheel, we could now cross sections of sand with relative ease, rather enjoying the strange floating motion of the tyres. (Although one of these brought Gareth down when he lost focus briefly!)

We averaged a steady twenty to thirty mph throughout the day but this varied as the surface changed. It was the rocks that were dangerous and which could burst a tyre, buckle a wheel or smash the bottom out of my engine if hit too hard. It was wonderful riding, though, the realisation that we were making our way, alone, across a section of the Sahara giving us a sense of freedom, of fulfilment.

Then, after riding for two hours or so, Gareth pulled up with a puncture. We unloaded the bikes, piled extra weight onto the rear to lift the front wheel off the ground, removed it and found the culprit: a large thorn had penetrated the tyre and tube. We fitted his spare. Looking at the stripped bike standing disabled on the vast desert plain, the wind gusting over us and blowing sand into everything made us feel rather vulnerable. Riding across this expanse of desert *reg* was exhilarating when everything was going well, but even this slight hitch suddenly made us aware of just how exposed and vulnerable we were. With the engines stilled, it was only the gusting wind and intermittent hissing of blown sand grains that peopled this vast emptiness with sound and emphasised our loneliness and isolation; the disabled bike without its front wheel, our bits and pieces strewn about the desert surface, gave the impression of a major accident. And there was no one about to offer assistance. We were entirely on our own.

New tube inserted, we re-fitted the wheel, packed up and set off again. But shortly after midday the same tyre went flat again. Another thorn had penetrated the tyre. Again we stripped off our luggage, removed the tube and replaced it with my spare. Later, Gareth confessed that at that time he began to feel a little concerned, began to doubt his GPS, wondering whether we would ever reach the tar road that we hoped was somewhere in front of us. But, at the time, he kept his fears to himself.

As the afternoon progressed, I was becoming tired. We paused to fill our tanks with the last of our petrol. The wind howled over the desert surface lifting grains of sand and turning the atmosphere a pale white. Gareth kept looking at his GPS and counting down the miles to the town of Al Mahbas, worrying that it wouldn't be there, that we would be stranded in this windy desolation, the tracks continuing on towards the horizon and our fuel running low.

Then, in the distance, we saw a pair of radio masts and knew we were safe. And suddenly the Al Mahbas-Zag tar road was in front of us. We mounted the soft bank onto its firm surface, relieved and yet deeply sad, pausing to look at the track we had been following for a day and a half continuing on into the wind-swept desolation until it disappeared into the heat haze on the horizon. We didn't want the adventure to end; both of us wanted to continue on, following the tracks until they led us somewhere deep in the desert.

But we had to move on. Our time in Morocco was drawing to a close and we needed to begin the long trek north. So, after resting a while and staring into the varied nothingness of stony sand and stunted bushes that had been our only companions for over a hundred miles, we reluctantly turned east and headed for the military town of Zag which we reached after about an hour.

Zag seems to be populated solely by men in uniform, but I'm sure it's not so. The military dominates everything and most men we saw were in uniform. The tension between Morocco and Algeria, the threat from the sporadic Islamic revolutions just over the border in northern Nigeria and Mali, is very real.

We asked for petrol.

There was none.

We rode up and down the main streets, stopping to ask pedestrians.

"Pas d' essence ..." and an indifferent shrug.

Finally a man knew of someone who had a store of petrol in a locked garage. He made some calls. We were led to a metal door behind which was a dusty pile of five-litre plastic bottles of various fuels. Relieved, we filled up then left this rather ugly town and continued to Assa where we booked into a hotel - tired, very dirty but feeling well pleased with ourselves.

There are no women in InIghem

Now for the long journey north.

We spent the next day riding across a flat barren plain from Assa, all the while being buffeted by a hot, dry wind blowing straight off the desert. The road was good - a thin strip of tar, breaking up on the edges, narrow enough for us to be pushed onto the dirt verge by passing buses and trucks. The road seemed to follow a range of low, dark-blue mountains, sometimes with soft collections of sand built up on the leeward slopes where the blown grains from the Sahara suddenly meet dead air and sink to the ground, their accumulations flowing with the gentle curves of dunes against the stark rocky mountainsides.

All the mountains in this part of Morocco seem to have been leant on by a giant hand at some time in pre-history, dipping the west-facing strata and lifting the east to an angle of about forty degrees. Later, though, when we finally left the N12 at Akka and headed into the mountains, it seemed as if this giant hand had stirred the strata with a spoon so that, at times, whole mountain ranges curled upon themselves in huge geologic swirls.

At last, we came again to the southern foothills of the Atlas, left the wind-blown desert flats behind and started to climb. The air turned cold and by late afternoon we were ready to look for somewhere to sleep the night. High up in the mountains we came upon the delightful town of InIghem and booked in to a small hotel, cheap (£5.00 each) but clean and, as usual, with a restaurant frequented by the local men all watching football on the large TV mounted high up on one wall.

Once we had unpacked, Gareth and I went for a cold walk around the town and into the cultivated land outside on rocky, terraced mountain slopes where wheat had begun to thrust its way through the stones. The icy wind drove us back to the hotel where we ordered coffee which we drank sitting outside overlooking the street. I was so taken by the atmosphere of this quaint little mountain town that I fetched paper and pen and began to write while the smells and sounds and sights, the people walking by were still close enough to touch:

There are no women in InIghem.

Or so it would seem.

We have been in this pretty little mountain town for two hours now and have not yet seen a woman. It's a male dominated society, Morocco.

"Cafés are the preserve of men," I observed to Gareth as we walked through the noisy public restaurant with its blaring football game dominating the room, the tables filled with men drinking coffee, men talking and watching the game.

"Everything here is the preserve of men," Gareth replied wryly.

I have not seen a woman sitting at a café table yet anywhere in Morocco. Not in the cities, of course, which are more Westernised, the women more liberated. But away from the cities, in the desert or mountain towns, it holds true: women seem to be rigorously controlled by their men folk. They - the men - sit at the white plastic tables and drink coffee or tea, prepared with ceremonial exactness, and chat and watch football on the telly (there is ONLY football on the telly in the street restaurants and cafes, all the time).

No women.

If you do occasionally see a woman, she will be making her way purposefully from one place to another, walking alone or with other women. It's the men who linger, who loll about, propping up walls, sitting at café tables, in doorways, watching life pass them by. It is the men who roam the streets with noisy bonhomie during the evenings.

Women in Morocco seem either to be hidden or walking somewhere with a purpose, veiled against the scrutiny of other males.

Little children of both sexes play on the sidewalks happily together.

But there are no teenage girls in Morocco. Trust me. As soon as the girls reach puberty they seem to disappear. It's as if they no longer exist. Hidden away, I assume, by jealously over-protective fathers inside thick-walled, dimly-lit rooms until ready for marriage.

The "tyranny of masculinity" I heard a liberated Moslem woman describe it once on a radio programme. And I believe she's right.

Young men roam the streets, probably eaten up by sexual frustration. We saw no flirting. Anywhere. No groups of teenage boys and girls hanging out, getting to know each other. It's as if girls somehow leap from being little children to mature women walking in tightly knit groups along the street with the intervening years surgically removed.

This is not a criticism. Just an observation.

Travelling in a foreign country you soon become used to observing things as they are, absorbing the unusual sights and sounds and accepting them as the norm for that country. But it was only when it suddenly became apparent to me: There are no women! *that I began to take note, actively to look for women (well, not in that way, of course), that the unnaturalness of it became apparent.*

But then you don't see overweight loutish, laddish women roaming the streets in drunken disarray in Morocco either. It's all about cultural or personal choice, I suppose.

Across the street a man sells pickled eggs from large plastic buckets; dishevelled cats range about our feet, desperate for love and affection; in the middle of the road dogs sleep, absorbing what is left of the day's heat. Cars drive slowly around them and they do not blink. Outside a butcher's shop, a haunch of goat hangs, an attached testicle - obligatory it seems - hanging with a faint air of reproach; next to the goat's leg, on a table, a cow's head sits, the neck ragged and bloody, the face looking somewhat sad and disappointed as if it hadn't expected its sudden demise.

We are the only foreigners here and the men watch us guardedly, their faces partially hidden behind the roughly woven cowls of their djellabas giving them the look of 16 [th] *Century monks on a pilgrimage. It's cold on the street at 9,000 ft. Outside town, the terraced mountain slopes are sprouting wheat, their tender green shoots emerging from between stones. Groves of pecan nut trees, just starting to bud, create patches of dark green against the rocks. Children walk past in the street and eye us shyly; one lifts a hand in greeting. They like the bikes because they are so big compared to the little pedal-assisted mopeds and small Chinese Docker buzz-bikes that are the poor man's transport here. We buy cashew nuts to eat with our evening coffee and oranges for tomorrow's ride from an indoor market, our purchases weighed on an old balance scale.*

Our hotel concierge, a dapper little man with thin, meticulously-trimmed moustache and silk waistcoat after the French style is solicitous, insists we park our bikes behind the locked gates of a friend's garage; the friend leads us there on foot and assures us it's no problem. The hotel is spotlessly clean and, although there is no douche, *we are directed, with an apologetic smile from our ever-solicitous concierge, to a communal basin in the corridor.*

I feel absorbed by this place with its icy winds from the bare, rocky mountains that surround us, its cowled, bearded men, the foreign sounds and smells that surround me.

And I still haven't seen a woman.

Not one...

That evening we sat in our cosy hotel room and perused the map. We needed to find something exciting to head for, something unusual and challenging. We didn't want our adventure to end in a whimper, a protracted ride along boring tar roads north and then across Spain and home. Looking closely at the map, Gareth found a small mountain road etched with black hatch marks; the legend informed us: *"Difficult and dangerous road".*

Gareth read this aloud, glanced up at me and I nodded. "Sounds good to me!"

But that was still a long way away. We decided to start heading into the High Atlas where Gareth wanted to ride as far up Mt Toubkal as we could, the highest mountain in North Africa at 4167 metres. There would be snow and at that time we were not sure we could get through but we wanted to give it a go. The

Polish bikers we had met in Laayoune on the coast had tried it a week or so before and had to turn back because of snowdrifts and find another route round.

At Akka we tried to get fuel but again there was nothing. We were directed to another metal door with the word *"Essence"* painted across in large roughly formed letters but it was locked and, despite a number of phone calls and a long wait, the owner couldn't be contacted. We had to head for Tata for fuel instead - sad because it caused us to miss an interesting pass over the mountains. But, looking at the map, we found another small road - fifty-five miles long - to Louziova and then on to Ounneine, which we decided to tackle on the morrow.

Tête-à-tête with Christina and Elka

The next day it took us seven hours to cover the one hundred and ten miles into the High Atlas following a narrow, winding pass from Aoulouz to Asni. The first sixty miles led us along the flat and rather uninteresting Tata River valley, a tributary of the Oed Draa, then we turned north onto the R203 and our speed slowed to about twenty-five mph as the narrow, potholed, crumbling strip of tar wound its way into the mist and snow above seventeen hundred metres; then, as we crossed onto the western slopes, the mist cleared and we rode under a deep blue sky.

The day was made more interesting by suicidal herds of goats, one of which Gareth nearly took out; a bunch of reckless Frenchmen driving Renault 4s, one of which nearly took Gareth out, and loose stones on the side of the road that did take me out.

It happened this way:

When a motorcyclist is leaning into a long outside corner and suddenly finds himself on loose stones, there is pretty much only one of two things he can do (other than pray, of course): He either keeps leaning into the corner on the marbles and falls over, or he straightens the bike, hits the brakes and prays he will stop sliding before he runs out of road. (Of course, if he hits the brakes while still leaning, he falls over.)

Riding blithely along, staring at the twisted and crumpled mountains that surrounded us, I briefly lost concentration on one of the fast outside corners and found myself in the loose gravel that accumulates on the verge of most roads, a drop of about ten feet - not vertical, but steep - into a rocky dry riverbed to my right. I straightened the bike and braked hard, sliding about eight metres in the loose gravel and wondering whether I would ever stop before I went over the edge.

I did. My front wheel had just started down, the back wheel slipped out and I dropped the bike and rolled rather ignominiously down the bank. Fortunately the bike held, half over the drop, caught somewhat tenuously by a very determined bush (unlike my BMW, a number of years before, which did *not* hold and ended up totally submerged in a river).

I dusted myself off and scrambled up the bank. I was unhurt, the bike undamaged - my spare fuel container and soft luggage having absorbed most of the impact. With the bike hanging half down the bank, I couldn't lift it but I knew that Gareth would be along soon when he discovered my absence behind him. I knew he'd like to have a good laugh at my expense (as I had done every time he dropped his KTM in the soft sand) and, anyway, why should I struggle to pick the bike up on my own when I had bred a son specifically to do things like that for me?

A short while later he appeared round the corner and laughed at me like a drain. We lifted the bike, repacked my luggage and set off again, realising just how close one always is to an accident when riding a bike.

We had hoped for more snow at the top of the pass but were disappointed. We paused only briefly to miss being killed by the many herds of fleet-footed goats that perversely left it to the last moment to cross the road in front of our wheels, leaping from the steep, rocky mountain sides onto the road and across before bounding away into the mist. That and when Gareth deliberately blocked the road with his bike in front of a rather puzzled young French driver. A group of French students were involved in some vintage Renault 4 rally across the mountains, travelling at silly speeds along very narrow, rutted tracks, shrouded in mist. Often the road had been cut out of bare rock with a steep drop-off on the one side and, especially around the hair-pin bends, only wide enough for one car to pass. When one nearly took Gareth out around a blind corner he decided to do something about it, deliberately driving his bike across the road as the next Renault 4 came roaring around a corner and shouting at the driver to slow down. As it wasn't him who had nearly taken Gareth out, I can just imagine his sense of perplexed hurt. Bloody Englishman, shouting at him for something he hadn't done!

Finally reaching Asni, we turned off onto a small road heading towards Mt Toubkal, hoping it would lead us above three thousand metres. As we wound our way up into the mountains, the snow-covered peak of Mt Toubkal occasionally appeared high above us through wisps of cloud. We picked our way through a small town, perched on the slopes of a mountain, the narrow road seeming to nudge its way between the two and three-story buildings which sometimes met overhead, held in place by arches. Most shops and boarding houses were clearly aimed at catering for the many hikers who flocked to this place from all over the world to climb Mt Toubkal. But we didn't stop; instead we pressed on, ever upward, hoping to reach above the snow line. Sadly, though, despite following a virtual goat track that wound its way into the mist, it finally ended at just over two thousand metres and we were forced to turn back.

On the way down, we stumbled upon a small lodge run by some very polite young local men and stopped for the night. Sharing the lodge with us were two young women, Elka, an Austrian, and Christina, a German - a physiotherapist and an osteopath - who had come to climb Mt Toubkal with a guide and mules to carry their luggage.

Gareth and I seriously considered taking a day off biking to climb the mountain as well but in the end decided against it. First, the area was very touristy with loads of day trippers heading off with their guides and luggage-carrying mules and, secondly, I didn't trust my damaged knee to cope with the climb.

That night, the girls and I having become chummy, we decided we'd eat our meal together. Picture the scene: Showered and reasonably clean, we make our way to the dining room, snug and cosy with its roaring fire perfuming the air with aromatic woodsmoke. The young ladies join us and tactile Christina chooses to sit next to me. We share a *tajine*, spooning the food onto our plates from the communal conical dish in the centre of the table. The girls listen with eager interest and expectation as Gareth and I relate fascinating anecdotes about our travels; they are amazed by our exploits. In turn, they share with us the difference between Austrians and Germans and tell us of their passion for ski-touring. The fire burns low. Elka remembers she has a hip flask of schnapps in her room; she fetches it and we drink the fiery liquid from the flask passed from one mouth to another in a spirit of flirtatious conviviality...

And I realise with a sense profound insight that I now know for certain that I am heterosexual.

Christina, sitting close to me, touches me on my arm and hand and thigh as she laughs in my ear her tinkling little laugh at the intelligent and amusing observations that I share throughout the evening and an electric current travels through my body at her tactile presence.

I never feel like that when *men* laugh with tinkling intimacy into my ear and brush their hands along my thigh. I'm more likely to be a little snappish and move to another part of the room.

Or maybe I'd just been travelling with Gareth for too long.

Encounter with a corrupt policeman

We left the next day, saying goodbye to our *entzückende junge mädchens,* whose mules were already loaded outside the hotel with their skis and belongings. From what we could hear from the balcony above them, they were engaged in an argument with their guide over the price they were being charged for the trip. The previous day their five-day excursion had unaccountably been reduced to three (for the same price, of course). Now, it would seem, the three hundred Dirhams they had agreed to pay the guide the day before had - again unaccountably - become five hundred. Such are the joys of being ripped off by the locals, skilled in the art from many years of practice.

Happy to have only ourselves to rely on, we loaded up and headed into the High Atlas, making for the Imilchil Gorge, highly recommended by other bikers we had met, as well as the travel guides. It was a roller-coaster ride of a day through the mountains; a snakes-and-ladders kind of day. We scrubbed the sidewalls of our tyres with eight hours of non-stop hairpin bends. If we'd had sliders on our knees, we'd have worn them down to the Velcro. (I'm exaggerating just a bit here.) We must have frightened the life out of a whole *kasbah* full of truck drivers that we met throughout the day on the apex of tight corners when we just couldn't lean over any more without lying the bikes down in the road, making their eyes suddenly become round and wide.

It was like that for eight hours - and we didn't need tickets.

At a brief lunch stop we met two Czech Republic bikers riding BMW GSs, both they and the bikes dusty and travel-worn. You could see they'd been off-roading in a big way. The more heavily built rider was obviously taking strain judging by the scabby sores around his mouth and his bloodshot eyes; the smaller one, slightly built and wearing glasses, seemed fully in control.

We took out our maps and it was clear that this guy knew what he was doing. We showed him where we had been and it was good to see the small expressions of approval on his face, the nods of the head when he traced our route. Then the questions like-minded travellers inevitably share: *How long did it take you? Much sand? How deep was the river? Any problems with the bikes? Did you hear about the guys who got ripped off by their guide?*

Their bikes were well prepared - oil coolers, sturdy crash bars and bash plates, soft luggage, nothing for show. They both wore full armour over light clothing, giving them both protection and coolness - ideal for riding through sand in the desert heat; much better than our hot, padded riding gear. The slighter guy had travelled Morocco a few times before and knew the country well. He suggested some roads we might think of taking in the direction of the gorge and marked one particular pass on our map that really sounded great - initially poor tar which became dirt as it crossed a high mountain range above the snow line.

Yes, thank you, we'll do that one.

It was good sharing with them, sensing their respect when we told them of our two-day desert crossing in the south - something they hadn't done.

After our break we set off again, riding fast but not dangerously, enjoying the lean of the bikes into the thousands of sharp corners as the road made its way through the mountains.

Until the policeman flagged Gareth down, that is. (He was in front at the time.)

We had been doing 83kph in a 60 zone.

We were philosophical: we must have broken the law a hundred times since entering Morocco - speed, crossing white lines. I'm not flaunting our breaking of the law: if you didn't cross a white line to overtake a slow truck in those never-ending mountains, you'd never get anywhere. White lines are painted almost non-stop along all roads through the mountain passes and, with the acceleration of the bikes, it is easy to nip past trucks moving at little more than walking pace. But to do it, you have no option but to cross a white line. Speed - well, it's difficult to keep to the speed limits when you're having fun and you haven't seen a policeman for a week (except the ones stopping you outside towns in the south, asking your occupation).

I stood back because it was Gareth who had been fined - although I later paid him my half; it could just as easily have been me had I been leading. Because of this I didn't become aware that Gareth had been hit on for a bribe until I saw my dear son reprimanding the policeman for dishonouring his badge and his uniform, telling him it was demeaning for a uniformed official, representing an honourable profession, to ask for bribes and he shouldn't do it again.

He almost prodded the man in the chest with his finger for emphasis. It was like listening to a disappointed teacher reprimanding a naughty child.

The policeman wasn't happy but there was no doubt he got the message.

It happened like this - and I've got to give it to our slimy policeman - it was a cleverly constructed and well-executed scam. He started off being excessively friendly, hail-fellow-well-met, telling us that he, too, was a biker, asking us how many times we had visited Morocco, telling us about his bike. Then he took Gareth to the police car and showed him our speed recorded on the camera, meticulously explaining the tariff of charges relating to various speeds - for our 83 kph in a 60 zone, Gareth would be required to pay five hundred Dirhams (about £50.00).

Now at this stage I had wandered off; Gareth told me afterwards that he took out his wallet and counted the five hundred Dirhams, which he put into the policeman's hand. The crooked bas***d then, with a smile and a friendly squeeze of the shoulder as he walked with Gareth towards his bike, peeled off three hundred Dirhams and thrust them into Gareth's pocket saying as he did so, "Because it's your first time in Morocco..."

Thinking about it, he was so clever. Instead of asking for a bribe of two hundred Dirhams to ignore the fine, he took the money and then gave some of it back, making it seem as if *he* was the one doing us a favour; that he was giving Gareth money instead of the other way round. And when someone presses £30.00 into your pocket and implies, "Here, this is a little gift from me as a favour because this is your first time visiting our wonderful country, aren't I kind?" one's natural response is to say, "Thank you."

But my son was too clever to be taken in by such chicanery, too principled to accept a bribe. He took the money out of his pocket, gave it back to the policeman and said, "No, thanks - I'll take the ticket."

The disgruntled officer of the law sat down in the back of his van and laboriously filled out the forms, not realising that he was about to have a strip torn off him for corruption.

It's not many young men who would hand back £30.00 and say, "I'll take the ticket, thank you."

Proud of you, my son.

We set off again, a little slower now. After six hours riding through the mountains we descended the eastern flank of the Atlas and, almost without recognising the change it occurred so quickly, we were back on the level desert plain, hot, flat, windy and bare. We pressed on for another two hours, following a dark, snow-capped barrier of mountains leaning over us to the east. Then, as the sun began to set, we finally stopped at a small hotel overlooking a running stream; on a far-off ridge, a mosque with its high, delicate minaret caught the late afternoon sunlight. We were the only guests and, later, we were served... yes, *tagine* for our supper.

The boy with desperate eyes

The next day we reached the Imilchil Gorge after a few hours' riding.

And what an anti-climax!

It had taken us two days of hard riding to reach the gorge but, the closer we came, the more tourists, camper vans, tour buses, caravans, hotels, restaurants and associated annoyances clotted the roads and landscape. It took only twenty minutes or so to ride up the steep-sided, rocky cleft which made its way through the mountains and I kept thinking: *There must be more to it than this, surely?*

We stopped at the top of the gorge at a hotel restaurant, built overhanging the cliffs and giving an excellent view of the engineering marvel of a road that winds its way through. Once again the place was packed with tourists; one repetitive, monotonous, highly annoying song was being played loudly on a loop over loudspeakers - the same song, over and over and over for the entire time we were there.

How I longed for the solitude, the silence, of the desert again.

A group of old men who had just got off a tour bus moved away from their wives and gathered round, as so often happens when we stop and people see our loaded, travel-stained bikes, drawn by the eloquent voice of adventure. They sidled up to us, peering at the bikes, our luggage, the GPSs then, tentatively, asked where we had come from and where we were going. We chatted briefly.

After twenty minutes Gareth and I couldn't stand the blaring repeated song a moment longer and headed off, onto the open road again. Within only a few minutes we had left the gorge behind, reinforcing the anticlimax. It had been nothing but a tourist trap. We climbed up onto the high ground where we could look down on the river winding its way through a steep-sided valley far below; ahead, the snow-capped mountains blocked the horizon in the direction we were heading. At least we had the prospect of following the small mountain road recommended by the two Czech Republic bikers.

A short while later we stopped on the side of the road to take photographs. A young lad approached me, holding out a rough, hand-made wooden tray on which he had laid a pathetic display of bits of rock and fossilised snail shells. I really didn't want to buy anything but the desperate, haunting look in his eyes and his obvious poverty touched me. How long had he been standing on the side of the road hoping some rich tourist would stop his car at this remote spot to look at the view? How many people had he approached with his meagre offering only to be brushed aside? Nothing he had to offer was anything like the glitzy crystals, the beautifully formed trilobites for sale at numerous tourist stalls along the road. Why would anyone pay money for the pitiful offerings he was holding out? But he had obviously scoured the rocky mountain slopes looking for the fossils that he hoped someone would buy, had found or made the tray he displayed them on. What goes through someone's mind as they stand on a bleak roadside day after day hoping a car will stop? What hope must rise in his breast when one eventually does? - and then to be waved away, his pitiful offerings looked at with disdain, the cars driving away and leaving him alone again amongst the rocks and the wind, seeing all the wonderful *things* in the cars that he cannot have.

I realise you who are reading this might be asking yourselves: What is he going on about? Of what significance is a Moroccan boy standing on the side of a remote road in the mountains to you?

All I can say is that he haunted me, the desperate longing in his eyes, his poverty, his yearning for me to buy something so he could take some money home. It reminded me of the old women selling forest-gleaned berries on the sides of remote Russian roads, hoping someone would stop and buy them.

Unable to disappoint him, to turn him away, I pointed to a small broken piece of rock on which was the delicate tracery of a fossilised fern - priceless and yet worthless. I didn't want it but asked him how much?

He crouched down and wrote "50" in the sand.

I turned away.

Immediately he cried out, "Twenty, twenty!" Snot shot out of his nose - a suppressed sob, I assume. He wiped it away on his sleeve, his eyes pleading with me, desperate.

I put ten Dirhams in his hand - what I was prepared to pay for something I really didn't want - and took a small piece of broken rock. He accepted the transaction blankly. Then I selected one of the many small, marble-sized fossilized snail shells he had on his tray and pressed more money into his hand.

He smiled. And as he looked at me, I believe at that moment he understood that I was doing it for *him*.

I hope so.

It made me feel a little less of the shit that I am, made me wish I could have the courage to do with my life what Jesus told the rich man to do: Sell all you have, give it to the poor and follow Me...

But, sadly, I don't have that courage...

We rode on, with thoughts of my worthlessness, my helplessness in the face of the poverty all around me, beating about in my head. What right have I to swan about on my fancy motorbike while blank-eyed children stand on the roadsides holding out their pathetic wares for me to ignore?

When you travel long distances on a motorbike, you get a lot of time to think inside your helmet. In a car you can chat, listen to the radio, play music. On a bike you are cocooned in your own little bubble and you have a lot of time to think. Deep thoughts, sometimes. "What's life all about?" thoughts. Sometimes I sing. I quote Hamlet's soliloquies with great depth of feeling. Have a little chat with God, reflect on the kind of person I have become...

Stuck in snow and mud

The Czech guys had told us of this small road, turning to dirt, that went right over a range of mountains close by and said we mustn't miss it. So that's where we headed, off the main road, away from all the tourists.

As they had described it, the tar road began to break up and, after about twenty miles, it reverted to dirt. We passed through small villages as we climbed, the road becoming the main street; little children, all jacketed and scarved, waved to us as we passed, their cheeks red from the cold and so cute I wanted to take some home as pets. Old men sat leaning their backs against the walls of mud houses, absorbing the weak rays of the sun and looking like extras from *The Life of Brian*. There were no shops, no restaurants, no hotels. The land, even the people, gave the impression that we were riding through the mountains of Tibet - and, strangely, when I mentioned it to Gareth, he said that he had thought so too. These rural people seemed to be from another race, with the snow-capped mountains rearing darkly above us.

And suddenly I felt my spirits lift; I felt as if I had come home; I was at peace here in these mountains, amongst these people in a way I could never feel in the hectic bustle of the towns, the endless blare of canned music, the calls of touts offering false friendship.

The going became slow and rough, fifteen to twenty mph rough. The track, about ten foot wide with no barrier, took us up the side of a mountain and I found myself gripping the handlebars, gritting my teeth and praying, "Please, Lord, don't let me go over the edge! Please, Lord -"

Half way up the side of this bare mountain we came across a bare-foot young man - late teens, perhaps - poorly dressed and with no warm jacket covering his thin shoulders. He called out to me, tried to wave me down, his eyes strangely blank.

I stopped and waited as he ran up to me.

He spoke with great earnestness but I couldn't understand him. We had no food with us except for the oranges we had bought a few days before so I dug them out.

He smiled when I gave him an orange. We ate together, the three of us on the windswept side of a mountain, an unspoken bond briefly uniting us through the shared food.

It's small, incidental things like that that one will never forget, that become part of the indelible memories of a trip: a bare-foot, blank-eyed boy high up the side of a mountain who smiled...

We continued up the side of the mountain, zigzagging our way up above three thousand metres. Other than the young lad, we had seen no one since we left the valley far below. Snow began to appear in rocky hollows above us and then on the road itself. The track became slippery, the bikes moving about strangely so that both Gareth and I thought we had punctures. So now we were riding along a wet, slippery track, with snow beginning to encroach onto the road, no barrier and the valley a very very long way below us. I found myself hugging the side of the track closest to the mountain and keeping as far as I could away from the drop. As we climbed further above the snow line, snow began to bank across the road until there was just a six-inch gap between the snow and the muddy edge of the track (OK, it wasn't a *vertical* drop by any means, but it was a l-o-n-g way down). We rode through one at a time, Gareth crossing the narrow gap standing on his pegs; I dabbed my way through, not taking any chances.

We finally reached the top at three thousand one hundred metres and then began the descent. All went well until we came around a corner and discovered that the whole road had been covered by a snowdrift. The snow was unmarked so obviously no one had come through that way for a while.

We dismounted and walked across; the snow was knee deep with hidden boulders underneath.

Gareth started his bike and had a go but almost immediately sank down to his engine. I got off my bike and made my way through the snow to help him. Together we tried to move the heavy KTM but it was stuck fast. Snow in front of the wheels had been compressed into ice and the wheels had wedged themselves between rocks somewhere deep under the snow. There was only one thing to do: unload everything to lighten the bike, dig the snow away from the wheels then, with Gareth pushing and controlling the throttle and me pulling on the front wheel, we managed to drag it across and out.

It's always easier the second time round. I unloaded my bike and took a higher route across, both of us pushing and pulling. When the bike started to bog down, being higher, I was able to angle down the side of the mountain and keep up the momentum until I was through.

Getting both bikes across that drift was exhausting and Gareth commented on how lucky we were that it was in snow, the air icy cold, rather than soft sand in the heat of the desert.

Thinking we were through the worst and on the downhill run to somewhere we could rest and eat, we set off down the pass, filled with a sense of achievement.

And then we hit the mud.

Now there's mud and there's mud. The ordinary stuff is OK, a biker can usually ride through it and not fall over. Then there's a certain type of mud especially designed by the Almighty to humiliate bikers and break their spirits, to bring them down to earth, as it were - literally and metaphorically. This mud does two things:

Firstly, you fall over, especially with a heavily laden, tall bike. It's so slippery that the rear wheel just spins without any forward motion, gives up and tracks sideways. It's like riding on wet glass. And even when you put your foot down to stabilise the bike, your foot slips out and you fall over. It's inevitable.

Secondly, the mud is like glue. It sticks to anything it touches and, if left, turns into cement after an hour or so. (That's why the locals build their houses with it.) You tread on it and suddenly you can hardly lift your leg because you've got half of the African continent sticking to your boot. Put your foot down again and you've got the *whole* of Africa sticking to your boot. But the problem is this: it sticks to tyres as well, so, within a few metres, you're riding with balloon tyres and all the gunk and stones and rocks and small trees that are picked up with the mud get stuck inside your front mudguard and any other orifice on your bike, large or small. These keep on packing themselves in there until the wheels lock solid. And you fall over.

Both Gareth and I dropped our bikes about six times in that five-mile stretch of muddy track. We crawled along, paddling the bikes through with our legs when it got particularly bad; we headed off road only to bog down in ground that was vaguely swampy; we scanned the road ahead for less slippery sections. We fell over. At one point I came across Gareth, covered in mud, his bike facing the wrong way. He'd reached a firmer section, accelerated, then suddenly found himself going sideways, the bike dropped and he slid along in the mud wondering when he and the bike would finally deign to stop. It was good for a laugh and a photo!

My front wheel eventually locked up at the top of a long steep downhill stretch. Gareth had kept his KTM going, keeping the front wheel turning by brute force (and cracking his mudguard mounts in the process) but my wheel locked solid. I thought, seeing that ahead of me was this long downhill track, I might just force the wheel round and it would, hopefully, clear itself - but it didn't. I tried twice, dropped the bike both times and rolled down the steep slope before scrambling back. (As any biker will know, if the front wheel is not turning, you fall over. It's a God-given law of motion - like Newton's Third Law of Thermodynamics. Or Boyle's Law. Or maybe I should have paid more attention in school.) There was no other solution: I had to remove the mudguard, clear out all the gunk and free the wheel.

As always happens in Africa, no matter where you stop, no matter how remote, after a few minutes a shepherd or herd boy will pop up from nowhere and watch you. As Gareth and I were working the spanners, an old man and his son, shepherds both, joined us. The father was warmly dressed, his clothes old and worn, his head covered with both woolly hat and faded blue *tagelmust*; his son wore nothing but a homespun smock like those worn by shepherds before the time of Christ. Both were bare foot but seemed oblivious of the cold. It wasn't long before they were helping.

We shared the last of our oranges with them. Their rough clothes smelled of smoke and damp. While we worked on removing the mud guard and clearing out the gunk, their sheep grazed quietly about us, cropping on the sparse, bristly tufts of grass that managed to survive so high up in the mountains.

Concrete-like mud scraped away, I loaded up the bike, strapped the mudguard on top with bungees and looked about for something to wipe the mud off my hands. Dotted about the barren slopes were what looked like smooth, rounded bushes. I walked up to one nearby and rubbed my hands over its surface despite a warning shout from the shepherd. Too late. I jabbed my hands into a million very sharp thorns. No wonder the sheep wouldn't touch them. We - the shepherd and his son and I - had a good chortle at my stupidity. I can imagine he supped quite a few beers on that little story: Stupid white man falling over with his big motor bike and rolling down the mountain and then trying to clean his hands on a thorn bush!

But then they don't drink beer in Morocco - do they?

We finally made it out of the mud and, on the floor of the valley, I stopped in the middle of a stream and tried to clean off as much of the solidified mud as I could; my radiator was completely blocked by about an inch of the disgusting stuff.

We set off again, tired now and looking forward to meeting the tar road, following a track along the bed of a narrow valley through which a clear stream ran amongst the stones. A few miles further we met a group of four *heavily* laden Slovakian bikers who were on their way up the track we'd just spent an age coming down, clean and fresh in their Touratec gear, massive aluminium panniers, top boxes and tank bags weighing the bikes down. The one guy had built a metal extension out the back of his bike and was carrying what looked like a *trunk* hanging off behind his rear wheel.

Why?

My travelling philosophy has always been: If you can't fit all your luggage in two unexpanded soft panniers, a small tank bag (for maps, glasses, and fiddly stuff) and a small top box, you're carrying too much. Look again and dump something. A wise motorcycle traveller once wrote: On any trip you can always adhere to this formula: Sort out your finances, pack up all your stuff and stare at it for a while. Now: *Double your money and halve your luggage.* Then go on your trip. You'll be fine...

This is good advice.

We all stopped, got off the bikes, took out the maps and had a chat: What's the road like ahead? Where're you going? Where've you been?

In a way, it was funny. There were we, bikes, clothes, exposed skin *covered* in thick, glutinous mud, knackered but fulfilled, speaking to this group of bikers, their big BMWs gleaming, all the trimmings - and all we could picture was them falling over in the mud, bogged up to their engines in snow. Their bikes were so heavy, so overloaded there was no way they would be able to pick them up alone. A few falls and their aluminium panniers would be mashed. And they *would* fall. There was just no way you could ride through that mud without dropping a heavy bike a few times.

We told them about the road ahead.

They didn't really believe us.

Gareth showed them some of our pics and told them how long it had taken us to get through - up the mountain and down the other side - four hours to cover twenty-five miles. We explained that the section of mud was only about five miles long and they could probably get around the snow drift by following sheep paths which we had seen about two hundred yards off to one side of where we had bogged down in the snow.

They had a little team talk. They raised their voices. Then they told us they were turning back.

We rode on and finally reached the tar road, exhausted but elated. It was one of the five highlights of our trip and more than made up for the disappointment of the tourist clogged Imilchil Gorge.

We were ready to head home now. We'd done three desert crossings, travelled deep into the mountains with the French guys and now crossed this wonderful pass, battling with snow and mud. We felt physically strong (a little worn out, but strong); the bikes had coped with everything we had thrown at them and were still handling perfectly; it was time to begin the one thousand five hundred mile return trip home.

Gareth was feeling hungry so we paused at a roadside cafe for a Berber Omelette - onion, peppers, tomato, raisins, about six eggs, whooo! - and then on thirty-five miles to El Ksiba, where we stopped at a most pleasant hotel built in the Moroccan style. We were the only ones there. The local couple who were employed to look after any guests who happened to stray into this remote region were so gracious towards us, offering to make us tea ("No charge -") while Gareth and I stripped our bikes down and tried to dig out the mud and rocks that had embedded themselves in every orifice and then hardened to concrete. I removed my front sprocket guard and discovered the chain was trying to force its way through cement-like mud and stones that had jammed themselves into every millimetre of space around the chain. Terrible stuff. Some had stuck onto Gareth's front forks, solidified and damaged the seals. I found and removed two rocks that had wedged themselves between the coils of my mono-shock.

After another *tajine* supper we slept the sleep of the just.

A village market day

After a good night's sleep, we loaded up the bikes having decided the night before when looking at the map that there was just one more narrow road over the mountains that we wanted to ride before resigning ourselves to the boredom of the tar road home.

So, again, we turned onto a small dirt track, a seventy-five mile detour that became yet another highlight of our trip. We again passed through small villages, little children laughing and waving as we passed, men in their hooded *jeballas* huddled against the cold, the high, barren landscape disappearing into the dark blues of the surrounding mountains.

By midday we reached a small village all a-bustle with activity. It was market day. We parked up, stripped off our heavy jackets and gloves and walked about amongst them, absorbing the atmosphere. We were the only "outsiders" there; we'd seen no other foreigners for seventy-five miles, just the two of us, a battered and potholed dirt/tar road, local people noisily going about their business - and, of course, the mountains. If I had had a thick skin and a fancy camera I could have taken a thousand National Geographic-type photographs and used them to publish a coffee table book.

But I kept my camera in my pocket. Sharing this moment, this space with the local mountain people was just too special. To take out a camera would have been an intrusion; it would have turned me into a tourist instead of a traveller, an observer of human kind.

Later, I wrote this while the memories were still fresh in my mind:

Donkeys, tethered with home-made rope, stand patiently in groups, empty panniers hanging loosely on their sides; chickens, piled together, their legs trussed with string, lie pathetically in the sun while others, by some quirk of fate, peck industriously between people's feet with blithe indifference; covered tables act as temporary butcher stalls where sheep and goats are slaughtered and chopped up with cleavers; sheep heads, bleeding and absurd, stare at us from the ground as we make our way past bloody piles of sheepskin, newly stripped from the still-warm bodies of slaughtered animals; a thump *and four lower legs complete with neat hooves are flung onto the ground in front of us; skinny dogs slink about, picking at the choicest bits; chunks of meat skewered on pieces of metal cook over smoky fires; a blackened kettle nestles in the charcoal next to a booth with plastic chairs and tables (for the men) who sit in the shade, drink tea poured ceremoniously into small glass cups. Gareth and I sit, absorbed into the group, and mime a request for tea. An old crone crouches in front of the fire, eyes half closed against the smoke, then lifts the kettle and pours the hot water into a battered aluminium teapot. Insulating her hand with a faded purple scarf, she brings it to us on a plastic tray. She smiles toothlessly when I pay her a few coins and shake my head when she offers change. She brings the scarf to the table, offers it with a shy smile when she sees me try to lift the hot teapot with my delicate white hands. I try to pour the tea from high up, directing the stream into the small clear glass cups like the Moroccans do but spill tea on the table. No one notices.*

Smoke blows into the tent from the fires outside, bringing with it the smell of cooking lamb. Chickens peck the ground under our chairs. We drink the scented tea heavily sweetened with lumps of rock sugar like the locals do, feeling strangely a part of the lives of these people, accepted by them somehow. Then we head back into the sun to walk about some more. Neither of us wants to leave, to break the spell; we want to remain, absorbed into the vibrant, colourful, noisy, raw life of these lovely people. We walk past wares for sale piled on the sides of the road: plastic shoes; tools, new and second hand; milk churns, buckets, braziers, tool boxes. Old men, hooded in their dun-coloured djellabas, cluster in small groups, catching up on the local gossip; a man sits behind a flat metal tray full of hot oil cooking vetkoeks. We buy two, sink our teeth into the hot, fatty dough and wish we'd bought more. Skeins of wool, brightly-dyed, and sold by weight, fill a shaded booth with a riot of colour; inside, an old man sits alongside his worn balance scale while women cluster around like children at a sweet-shop window, trying to decide what to buy.

But eventually we have to move on. We don our riding gear and reluctantly head down the road, away from this special place, our clothes smelling of wood smoke, the sweet taste of tea still in our mouths. And as I ride, I think about how I would like to tell all my biker friends about the remote places we have travelled through over the past two days, encourage them to ride here and experience what we have experienced. But then another part of me wants to keep it to myself, hide it from the world, keep the tourists away because, how long before faux Moroccan kasbahs spring up alongside these remote roads and men in brightly-coloured djellabas start waving you to one side and offering a "Mountain Experience"?

I don't want these gracious, gentle people to be changed by the blight of tourism. But, then, even our passing will have changed them in some way...

Should I have waved away the change she was about to give me? Should I have bought, however reluctantly, the fossils from the dusty bare-foot boy on the side of the road, shared oranges with the shepherd and his son in the mountains? Can one pass through a country and *observe* without having an effect on the people one observes, changing them by our very presence?

Taken to extremes, should we, as travellers, be like the naturalists who will watch an elephant die of thirst in the Kalahari, a baby baboon die of hunger because blood-sucking ticks have so clogged its nostrils that it cannot breathe and suck - because to do so would be an interference in the natural order of things, would be a placing of one's thumb on the scales of life, interfering with natural selection?

Personally I would rather pick away the ticks from the baby baboon's nose and allow it to suckle, give the dying elephant water to drink. I'm a part of Nature too; why should positive intervention from me not counter negative intervention from some other part of the natural world, like drought or pests?

Perhaps it's because our intelligence and power enable us to manipulate - or even destroy - the world completely, counteracting the slow, methodical process of evolution - in the same way that inhabitants of rich, powerful countries will always overwhelm and eventually dominate the poorer people they rub against, changing them rather than being changed by them, seldom for the better.

As I travel, I am very aware that, in trying to escape the very places others flock to, I too am leaving my footprints on the lives of those with whom I come into contact. I just pray the impressions I leave in the soil of their lives will be good ones.

"First do no harm - " the Buddhist philosophy sounds about right. Similar, in a way, to Jesus' "Do unto others as you would have them do unto you".

These ramblings might sound solipsistic and, in a way, they are. But these are the thoughts that ran around inside my head, inside my helmet, for hours after we had left that small market-town village, its people going about the business of their daily lives, the way we had brushed so lightly against them in passing; the shepherd and his son high up in the mountains; the blank-eyed, bare-foot young man who smiled...

For the rest of the afternoon we rode across the green, fertile plain between the Atlas Mountains and the coast, becoming increasingly built-up and clogged with life and industry so very different to the pure, uncluttered landscape of the mountains, until we reached the bustling city of Meknes where we stopped for the night.

The next day we woke to our final day in Morocco and headed for Ceuta and the Spanish border.

It started to rain.

Yes, I thought, our trip started with four days of rain and, just to even things up as it were, the travelling gods are going to make sure it ends with rain.

We crossed the border into Spanish territory without hassle, rode straight onto the ferry to Algeciras where we found a cheap hotel just opposite the terminal (so cheap, in fact, that there was no soap in the bathroom - but we did find a partially used piece left by a former guest as well as an unused sachet of shower gel). I used both to wash my hair, then rubbed my Sahara-stained shirt on my head to make the most of the soap. No matter how hard I had scrubbed the shirt over the past week, it remained a delicate shade of desert orange.

When we take off our clothes in the evening, the room is filled with the flavour of ripe cheese.

And so, the long ride home across Spain, through intermittent rain and cold, blustery winds - two fast, three-hundred-mile days along very good roads that we often had entirely to ourselves. The collapsing Spanish economy must be biting deep. On the surface, though, everything still looks prosperous. But then I saw a man, who could have been my next-door neighbour, sitting on the pavement behind a torn piece of cardboard on which had been hand-written: *Sin resources - Gracias.*

As I gave him a handful of coins, that feeling of uselessness came over me again. The coins I gave him were for *me,* not for him, I know that.

Around the corner a well-dressed woman opened a charity bin, leant over so she was almost inside and rummaged around for someone else's unwanted clothes.

It seems the poor are not only found in the mountains and the desert...

...ooOoo...

If you're interested, here's the link to photographs and our route on Google Earth again: http://www.hareti.co.uk

My email address if you'd like to ask any questions or comment on the trip: lgbransby@hotmail.com

Other books by Lawrence Bransby:

Adult Novels:

Life-Blood - Earth-Blood
A Matter of Conscience
Second Sailor, Other Son

Travelogues:

A Pass too Far
Travels in Central Asia
Trans-Africa by Motorcycle
A Father's Diary
There are no Fat People in Morocco
Venture into Russia
Three Motorcycle Journeys
The Wakhan Corridor
By Motorcycle through Vietnam
Reflections on a Gracious People
A Walk to Lorenco Marques
Reminiscences of a 13-year-old
By Bicycle to Beira
Reminiscences of a 15-year-old
Plymouth-Dakar/Banjul Old Bangers Challenge

Novels for Young Adults:

Down Street
Winner of the MER Prize for Youth Literature
Remember the Whales
Winner of the J.P. van Der Walt Prize
A Mountaintop Experience

Book Chat South African Book of the Year 1993
Homeward Bound
Shortlisted for the MNET Prize
The Geek in Shining Armour
Of Roosters, Dogs and Cardboard Boxes
The Boy who Counted to a Million
Winner of the Sir Percy Fitzpatrick Prize;
MNET Award Finalist '96
Outside the Walls

Printed in Great Britain
by Amazon